Using
RUBRICS *for*
Performance-Based
Assessment

Using RUBRICS for

Performance-Based Assessment

A Practical Guide to Evaluating Student Work

Todd Stanley

Routledge
Taylor & Francis Group

NEW YORK AND LONDON

Library of Congress catalog information
currently on file with the publisher.

First published in 2019 by Prufrock.Press Inc.

Published in 2021 by Routledge
605 Third Avenue, New York, NY 10017
2 Park Square, Milton Park, Abingdon, Oxon OX14 4RN

Routledge is an imprint of the Taylor & Francis Group, an informa business.

© 2019 by Taylor & Francis Group

Cover and layout design by Allegra Denbo

ISBN: 9781032142166 (hbk)
ISBN: 9781618218674 (pbk)

DOI: 10.4324/9781003239390

Table of Contents

Introduction

The Unintended Consequences of SMART Goals

As anyone who has spent any time in education knows, there are movements that come with the field. For example, among others, there is the standards movement, the small schools movement, the college- and career-ready movement, and the movement of integrating technology into the classroom. Beyond these, one prominent movement throughout the past decade has been the educational data movement. The essential question of the data movement is "What data can you show me to prove that students are learning?" In the past, educators depended on subjective measures, such as grades, teacher recommendations, and graduation requirements, to determine whether a student was succeeding or not. Now the expectation is that objective measures will show educators whether a child is really learning. The goal is to convert the measurement of mastery into a quantifiable number that will prove whether or not a student is growing as a learner.

Part of this movement led to the use of SMART goals (The Mind Tools Content Team, n.d.) in education. These are goals that are:

- ✓ S—specific,
- ✓ M—measurable,
- ✓ A—achievable,
- ✓ R—realistic, and
- ✓ T—time related.

The idea behind SMART goals is to conduct an assessment that can measure growth. If the assessment determines that a student is not growing as a learner, then practices are put into place to help him or her do so.

Different groups use SMART goals to measure their success. For instance, businesses use SMART goals to increase profits, improve customer service, and increase efficiency in business operations. The medical field can look at patient visits, quality of care, and health outcomes. Sports teams use SMART goals to make players more effective, improve statistics, and set goals to improve wins. If these goals work for such organizations, why would education not want to use such a system—especially if it is going to improve student achievement?

These goals can be used at various levels of an educational organization, from the central office setting big picture goals for the district, to schools measuring the building's success on particular skills, to individual teachers trying to demonstrate the growth of their students, to even having students set their own SMART goals as they persevere toward new achievements.

For example, a teacher might use SMART goals in the classroom by giving a class a math test. One student misses questions 2, 4, 7, and 11, all of which have to do with fractions. This might indicate to the teacher that this student needs more intervention with fractions, so the teacher works with the student further, breaking concepts down into more understandable chunks and providing more practice. If several students in the class show a similar pattern, the lesson on fractions may need to be retaught to the whole class. On the other hand, the results of the test might show a teacher the areas in which a student displays strengths, which would hopefully inspire this teacher to find ways to challenge the child by learning about the concept in more depth.

SMART goals sound great, but here is the problem: SMART goals seek to get to an unbiased, cold hard fact that indicates the mastery of a student. Either the student mastered the objective or he did not. How black and white can you get? To make the evaluation of mastery as objective as possible, providing questions with one correct answer seems logical. This eliminates the subjectivity of open-ended questions that have multiple possible answers and are subject to interpretation. Having one correct answer to a question avoids the problem of one teacher evaluating a student's response one way, while another teacher might see things differently because there is so much discrepancy in what may be considered mastery-level work. This is why most state assessments use mostly, or all, multiple-choice questions—because the testing coordinators do not have to train evaluators to be as unbiased as possible.

In the classroom, this might involve a teacher writing a 10-question multiple-choice test to determine whether students understand proper sentence structure. One student gets eight of the questions correct. This student displays mastery of the skill, perhaps only requiring a brief review of the two missed questions. Another student gets only three of the questions correct, showing a lack of mastery of the skill, requiring intervention. These examples are objective uses of data. A multiple-choice test is easy and quick to grade—the answers are clear.

Although this is the ideal way to assess mastery in an ideal world, and certainly the easiest, there are certain skills that are more difficult to objectively measure, such as public speaking. After all, how does one rate a student in public speaking? If you are rating a performance, there is a lot of interpretation that can take place. One person might think the student spoke very well, while another might have seen some issues. Because this rating is based on opinion, many would argue that this type of assessment does not invoke the tenets of SMART goals. Otherwise, everyone who evaluated this student would decide the same result. Also, the amount of time it takes for the student to give his or her speech and for the evaluator to rate it is much more involved than other more objective forms of assessment—and time is one of those things in today's world of content standards that teachers do not have a whole lot of. So, if you are trying to create an objective and easy-to-grade assessment, a logical choice would be a multiple-choice test. A student could have the following question on an assessment:

> Which of the following is the best way to present a speech to a crowd?
> a. Reading from your notes word for word
> b. Speaking to one spot on the wall
> c. Glancing around the room in a fidgety manner
> d. Scanning the room while talking, occasionally making eye contact

If a student selects D, then he or she would be correct. The problem is this: that knowledge does not make the student a good public speaker. If a teacher truly wants to assess this skill, the student is going to have to actually give a speech to an audience and be evaluated on how effective his or her speaking skills are.

This is the problem for the so-called "soft skills"—they are challenging to assess. For example, three people might watch a student's speech, and one may think the speaker did a really good job, one may think the speaker did an average job, and the third may think the speaker was not very good. The three audience members might be evaluating different things. There is no right or wrong answer, black or white choice, or mastery/nonmastery option. There is a lot of gray area. There are many qualities of presenting a good speech, some the student might do well and other aspects that may need a lot of improvement. How do you assess mastery if there are so many factors involved? To put it simply, the biggest challenge is that there is too much subjectivity in evaluating skills such as this.

You could conduct an assessment that better defines what good public speaking looks like and what the evaluators should be looking for, but this is harder. If I tasked you with writing a multiple-choice test or writing a comprehensive rubric, which one would take you more time and effort to complete? Because of the subjectivity of the rubric, there is some doubt cast as to whether the skill being measured aligns with a SMART goal. After all, SMART goals are supposed to be specific as well as measurable. Creating an objective assessment that properly evaluates these harder-to-measure skills is quite a challenge. This challenge causes a lot of educators to simply take the easy way out and no longer evaluate these skills.

Consider the difference between a multiple-choice assessment and an essay assignment. There are few educators who would argue that multiple-choice responses provide a clearer picture of whether a student understands a concept or not than an essay. After all, on a multiple-choice assessment, there are only three to four choices students must contemplate, and the correct answer is right there in front of them. There's also the luck factor—a student has a 25% chance of guessing the correct answer. Guessing on an essay question is difficult. A student has to have basic understanding in order to address an essay assignment. Thus, an essay provides a more extensive and detailed look at whether a student has indeed mastered a particular concept or skill. Unfortunately, administering an assessment often comes down to time, that precious commodity that teachers often do not have enough of. If I have a classroom of 30 students, and I administer an assessment with three essay questions on it, suddenly I have to read 90 essays, all of varying length. This is going to take longer than a single planning period. If, however, I give those same 30 students a 20-question multiple-choice assessment, I have considerably cut down the amount of time needed to grade. Because this is the easier path, hard-to-measure skills that require a rubric or more of a time commitment simply get passed over. Instead, we measure those skills that fit into the easy mold of a SMART goal—usually the memorization of content.

First, let me be clear. There is nothing wrong with assessing students' understanding of content. It serves as the building blocks to higher level conversations. The problem is when content is the only focus of the learning. The unintended consequence is that, because content is knowing a specific fact or method for solving a problem, students then play the memorization game. They memorize the content without understanding the context and when the information should be used. That is where the soft skills come into play. How can you adapt the content in an authentic, real-world situation so that students are not just memorizing the content, but learning it at a much deeper level that will lead to an enduring understanding?

Oftentimes, soft, 21st-century skills, such as . . .

- ✓ public speaking,
- ✓ collaboration,
- ✓ creativity,

- ✓ critical thinking,
- ✓ adaptability,
- ✓ leadership,
- ✓ problem solving,
- ✓ grit,
- ✓ initiative, and
- ✓ global and social awareness

. . . get left in the dust or are unintentionally overlooked. There are few people who would argue against the importance of such skills. Educators are aware that students who are skilled in these areas will be much better equipped in the real world than students who only have facts and content memorized. Despite this, many educators focus on the content because that is what is easy to measure and can be quantified into a number, letter grade, or SMART goal.

The ultimate examples of this are Advanced Placement (AP) tests. AP is a national program created by the College Board that offers college-level classes to high schoolers. When a student takes an AP course, in most cases, no matter what the student's effort is, no matter how well he or she does with ongoing assignments, no matter how good his or her body of work for the class is, the student's actual results all come down to the AP Exam. If a student comes to class and does not ever use the skills needed to pass a college course, such as initiative, grit, critical thinking, problem solving, collaboration, adaptability, or creativity, he or she could still receive college credit if he or she sits for the exam and scores a 3 or higher. Typically, more than 50% of an AP exam is made up of multiple-choice questions—those easy-to-measure, content-heavy responses. Many AP courses are very heavy in content but not very focused on 21st-century skills.

In using mostly easy-to-measure assessments, educators lose the power of performance assessment. If you think about the areas in your life in which you are evaluated, whether it be your work, your parenting, or your hobbies, you are giving a performance. For instance, as an educator, teaching is a performance. You are not evaluated on how well you answer a multiple-choice test at the end of the year. You are evaluated on how your students do on the end-of-year test. This is predicated on the fact that you have been performing all year, trying to get your students to understand the content they are going to see on their test. You are also evaluated based on observations in the classroom. Teaching, itself, is a performance assessment.

Performance assessments also address the boredom factor. Grading a multiple-choice assessment is, indeed, usually quicker, but how exciting is that? Going through and checking the answer key to see whether students marked the correct response can be very tedious and mind-numbing. Performance assessments are usually more engaging, not only for the students, but also for teachers. Seeing what your students have learned in your class unfolding in front of you in the form of a presentation, a model, or a well-written paper is far more rewarding than admiring the numbers or letters in a gradebook.

Why is it so terrible that these soft skills are getting overlooked? First off, why are they referred to as soft skills? *Hard skills* refers to the specific content that is being taught in each content area. Soft skills, however, are defined as:

> the personal attributes, personality traits, inherent social cues, and communication abilities needed for success on the job. Soft skills characterize how a person interacts in his or her relationships with others. (Doyle, 2018, para. 5)

These do not seem to be "soft"—they seem like the skills everyone must possess in order to be successful in the adult world. They are the glue that brings all of the hard skills together. After all, what good is a hard skill if you cannot communicate it effectively, or if you cannot get along with someone long enough to utilize the hard skill? Some people prefer to use the term *21st-century skills* to refer to these softer skills. There are also a couple of issues with this terminology. First of all, we are a couple of decades into the 21st century. Any child you have in your classroom has known nothing but the 21st century. Another issue is that these are skills that were just as useful in the 18th century and will continue to be important into the 22nd century.

Wagner (2008) used a more appropriate term in his book *The Global Achievement Gap*. He called these "soft" skills *survival skills*. This term is much more fitting for these skills because, without them, students will struggle in the real world. Students can survive not knowing how to determine the square root of a number. They cannot survive without knowing how to research something or find information (information literacy) or being able to think critically. After talking to many global business leaders, Wagner arrived at the following skills that employers are seeking:

1. critical thinking and problem solving,
2. collaboration across networks and leading by influence,
3. agility and adaptability,
4. initiative and entrepreneurialism,
5. effective oral and written communication,
6. accessing and analyzing information, and
7. curiosity and imagination.

By focusing too intently on developing SMART goals, we are not teaching these survival skills to our students. Wagner (2008) learned from business leaders that the skills they were seeking and expecting from new hires and entry-level applicants were not the skills students were learning in their traditional classroom settings. The United Negro College Fund used to have the slogan, "A mind is a terrible thing to waste." Guess what? So is an opportunity to educate someone in survival skills. If SMART goals and content mastery are causing teachers and schools to no longer address survival skills in their classes, then we are not properly preparing our students for real life—where these skills are far more valued than a person's ability to remember content.

This is especially important for our students, as many jobs that will be available for our forthcoming graduates have not even been created yet. How do you give students the content needed to work a job that does not exist yet? The answer is that we cannot. We can, however, teach our students survival skills that will allow them to succeed no matter what line of work they pursue.

That is the point of this book—to help you to be able to measure these critical survival skills so that they are not overlooked in the classroom. How does one do this? By writing objective rubrics that will enable you to properly determine mastery of these important survival skills. Chapter 1 describes what a rubric is, how it can be used, and why it can be used. This is followed by a rationalization of the importance of using rubrics both for the student and the educator. Chapter 3 looks at various types of rubrics, how to match the appropriate rubric with an assessment, and how you want students to display mastery. We must answer the essential question about the difference between being valid and being reliable, and how you ideally need to consider both of these factors when creating a rubric. The heart of the book is Chapter 5, where you are taken through, step-by-step, how to construct a reliable and valid rubric that will properly assess a hard-to-measure skill. The next chapter provides examples of rubrics that are either invalid or unreliable and what can be done to fix them. Once you get the hang of writing good rubrics, you will want to pass this skill along to your students. Chapter 7 shows the value in doing that and how it can be done. Once you have a rubric completed, how do you grade with it? Chapter 8 looks at concepts such as effective feedback and how to communicate the results of a rubric with students. The final chapter shows how to develop rubrics to assess some of those seemingly unmeasurable skills, those survival skills. The conclusion then challenges you to create your own rubric to evaluate this very book.

Assessing the Chapter

The end of each chapter features a rubric for you to review what the chapter was about and determine its value to your professional development. This first rubric (see Reader Assessment 1 on the following page) is a visual one that is intended as a self-assessment regarding your excitement about this book.

READER ASSESSMENT 1

How excited are you about this book after reading the introduction? Rate yourself by identifying with the proper emoji.

😍	I am totally stoked to continue reading—positive that this book will change the way that I teach.
😊	I am very excited to continue reading—pretty sure that this book will help me somehow in the classroom.
😊	I am a little excited about continuing—still need another chapter or two to be convinced.
😁	I am somewhat excited—kind of on the fence about whether this book will be valuable for me or not.
😮	I am wondering if I made a mistake by purchasing this book, but hoping to be proven wrong.
😭	I am sad that I paid money for this— wondering what the refund policy is.

Chapter

1

What Is a Rubric?

Before we can get into constructing objective rubrics that assess hard-to-measure skills, it is important to both understand and determine what a rubric is. A rubric, in its simplest form, is merely an established criterion for assessing the mastery of outlined skills and/or content. To put it even simpler, a rubric shows you what an assignment would look like if it were done right, and also what it would look like if there were areas that needed improvement. In a deeper sense, a rubric is like a blueprint. Architects make blueprints so that other people can build structures, such as a house. An architect designs the house, where fixtures might go, where to put walls, and how big or small each element of the construction needs to be. Someone else, however, builds this house, so the blueprint needs to be clear enough that someone who had nothing to do with its creation knows what he or she is doing while using it. If the blueprint is done well, the builder can construct the house exactly like the architect intended. The same applies to a rubric. A teacher makes a rubric to act as a blueprint for his or her students. If the students do what is asked of them in the rubric, they will have shown mastery of the skill the rubric intends to evaluate. And just like the blueprint for a builder, if students do not follow the rubric, there is the possibility that there will be problems with the finished product—perhaps even a shaky foundation.

A rubric is also a guide for the rater—in most cases, the teacher. The rubric clearly defines what good work look likes and, equally important, what poor work looks like. The rubric should be descriptive rather than evaluative. That is not to say that it cannot be used to evaluate a performance, but that the rater should "match the performance to the description rather than 'judge' it" (Brookhart, 2013, p. 4). The rater should determine how each aspect of a student's performance fits into the descriptions outlined in the rubric. Figure 1 is a snippet from a rubric that shows what descriptions might look like. The example is from a rubric for a mock museum exhibit, in which students were tasked with creating an exhibit to show what they learned during a sixth-grade unit about the Egyptians.

Clear descriptions are used to help the rater visualize what the final product should look like at various levels. For instance, for the description of the display, not only does the rubric use the word "professional," but also it lays out what this professionalism would look like, "like an exhibit that would appear in a real-life museum." These types of descriptions continue on the next two levels, comparing the middle range of performance to "a high-quality school project," and not looking professional to "like no time or effort was put into its creation." Each of these descriptions can be visualized by the rater, as he or she is likely to have seen examples of all three of these in his or her experiences.

Formative and Summative Rubrics

Rubrics can be both formative and summative. A formative rubric shapes or forms students' learning. It is used to monitor the students' learning process. The rubric is not written in stone or meant to be an end-all, be-all. Instead, a formative rubric is designed to be revisited, added to, altered, and changed. Take, for example, Figure 2, which is a rubric for social and emotional learning.

You could use this rubric to determine a student's level of understanding of social and emotional skills. Notice that these levels are synonymous with Webb's (2002) depth-of-knowledge (DOK) levels. The lower skills are simply knowing the skill, which is a DOK 1 of recall. The intermediate skills call for applying this skill, or DOK 2, while the higher skills ask students to make conscious decisions or think about them and use them appropriately, which is DOK 3.

A teacher might use this rubric at the beginning of the lesson and determine that a student is simply in the lower skills. As the lesson progresses, however, the student begins to not only know, but also perform, the skill, moving him or her into the intermediate skills. And then the teacher is walking down the hallway one day and sees the same student counseling an upset friend, demonstrating the higher level of skills. This rubric could be used throughout the lesson—and beyond—to determine the growth of the student.

A summative assessment, on the other hand, is usually not recording the process and progress of a skill, but rather the culmination of learning said skill. For instance, let us say that a student has been tasked with delivering a presentation.

Display
✓ Display looks professional—like an exhibit that would appear in a real-life museum.
✓ Display clearly captures the three ideas it is meant to.
✓ Display is easy for people to view, showing many details about the ideas.
✓ Display looks somewhat professional—like a high-quality school project.
✓ Display captures most of the three ideas it is meant to, but leaves a few parts out that should be included.
✓ Display can be viewed, but some details are difficult to see.
✓ Display looks unprofessional—like no time or effort was put into its creation.
✓ Display does not capture the three ideas it is meant to, causing confusion.
✓ Display is not easy for people to view, leaving out many details about the ideas.

FIGURE 1. Example rubric descriptions.

Above-average Skills	✓ Makes conscious decisions to use the skill appropriately ✓ Understands how one's behavior is influenced by other factors ✓ Is ever increasing the probability of using the skill effectively
Average Skills	✓ Can perform a rough approximation of the skill ✓ Has become fluent in executing the skill ✓ Is consistently shaping the strategies through practice
Below-average Skills	✓ Knows the steps and strategies that make up the skill ✓ Knows the information that is important to the skill ✓ Knows the vocabulary used in the skill

FIGURE 2. Example rubric for social and emotional learning. Adapted from Marzano, 2015.

The rubric would not be used throughout the process other than as a blueprint for what the final product should look like. The rubric is used when the student gives the final performance. It might look something like Figure 3, which is a rubric designed to evaluate a group project and presentation about a world religion.

The teacher would have this rubric in front of her as the students were giving the presentation, marking what is present and what is not in the performance according to the descriptions in the rubric. The rubric does not assess the effort of the students throughout the preparation of the presentation. It simply assesses the final product, which is what makes it summative.

Word Religions Presentation

Students:_____ Religion:_____

Overall	Content	Presentation	Maps
Excellent (A)	✓ Students include many details and examples to support their claims. ✓ Research is from reliable sources. ✓ Interview adds much to the presentation, giving perspective to the religion.	✓ PowerPoint flows well. ✓ PowerPoint uses meaningful visuals that add to the content of the presentation. ✓ Speakers present clearly, without reading the PowerPoint to the audience.	✓ Presentation includes five maps that clearly show the progress of the spread of the religion. ✓ Presentation includes a map/chart indicating where the religion is practiced widely today, including statistics about the number of followers.
Good (B–C)	✓ Students have a few details and examples to support their points, but could use more. ✓ Most of the research is from reliable sources, but some is questionable or incorrect. ✓ Interview is included and provides some information about the religion, but it doesn't really add anything to the presentation.	✓ PowerPoint jumps around some, making it hard to follow at times. ✓ PowerPoint uses visuals, but not all of them are meaningful; some are just there for decoration, rather than expanding knowledge. ✓ Speakers present clearly most of the time, but every once in a while read the presentation to the class.	✓ Presentation includes 3–4 maps that show where the religion spread and how. ✓ Presentation includes map/chart showing places where the religion is practiced widely, but does not include statistics about the number of followers.

FIGURE 3. Example summative assessment rubric.

Overall	Content	Presentation	Maps
Needs Improvement (D–F)	✓ Students do not use details and examples to support their claims. ✓ Much of the research comes from questionable sources or is incorrect. ✓ Interview is not included or presents only a stereotype of the religion.	✓ PowerPoint is so disorganized it is difficult to determine what is being spoken about. ✓ PowerPoint lacks visuals, or most of them add nothing to the content. ✓ Speakers read the entire presentation or do not make themselves clearly heard.	✓ Presentation includes two or fewer maps that show the progress of the spread of the religion. ✓ Presentation does not include a map/chart indicating where the religion is practiced widely today.

FIGURE 3. Continued.

There are times, however, when a rubric can be both formative and summative. Take, for example, Figure 4, a rubric for assessing a research paper about Westward expansion. This rubric could be used by the teacher to generate a summative evaluation at the end of the lesson, indicating what grade a student earned with her cumulative research paper. The student could also use the rubric prior to turning in the assignment in order to refine it and fix mistakes. The student can either go over the paper herself using the rubric or ask a peer to do so. By doing this, the student learns where she is in the learning process, making efforts to close any gap should she recognize it. For example, using the rubric, the student could look over her paper and realize that she does not provide many examples throughout. Given the descriptor, "Student provides plenty of examples to support statements made in the paper," the student reviews her research and adds an example for every statement she makes. The student has then used the rubric to learn how to properly write a research paper. The rubric formed the student's learning process. The teacher also can use this same rubric when the student turns in her research paper. The teacher can use the rubric to create a cumulative evaluation, giving the student a final grade for the unit, making it a summative assessment.

Westward Expansion Paper			

Student:_____   Religion:_____

Overall	Outline	Research	Grammar/Sentence Structure
Excellent (A)	✓ Paper follows the outline clearly, allowing the reader to understand what is discussed at any given time ✓ Student provides plenty of examples to support statements made in the paper ✓ Student provides much detail, explaining concepts and ideas so that the reader can gain a full understanding of what is discussed	✓ Research is consistently paraphrased/put into student's own words ✓ Research/citations come from a variety of sources; student does not rely heavily on one resource ✓ A primary source and direct quotes from it are used in the paper to add to its depth	✓ Paper has few to no spelling/grammatical errors ✓ Paper is typed in the correct format, using double-spaced, 12-point Times New Roman ✓ Paper uses sentence structures that make the paragraphs flow and easy to read
Good (B–C)	✓ Paper follows the outline, but doesn't always allow the reader to understand what is discussed at any given time ✓ Student gives examples to support statements made in the paper, but inconsistently ✓ Student provides detail, explaining concepts and ideas, so that the reader can gain an understanding of what is discussed	✓ Research is paraphrased/put into student's own words, but student occasionally uses terms and phrases that are not his or her own ✓ Research/citations come from a variety of sources, but student relies on one source for much of the information ✓ A primary source and direct quotes from it are used in the paper, but they do not add depth to the paper	✓ Paper has the occasional spelling/grammatical errors, including more than a handful of mistakes ✓ Paper is typed but not always in the correct format; there are inconsistencies in font, size, style, or spacing ✓ Paper mostly uses sentence structures that make the paragraphs flow and easy to read, but occasional awkward sentences cause confusion

FIGURE 4. Example formative and summative assessment rubric.

Overall	Outline	Research	Grammar/Sentence Structure
Needs Improvement (D–F)	✓ Paper does not follow the outline, causing confusion for the reader ✓ Student provides few to no examples to support statements made in the paper ✓ Student does not provide much detail, leaving the reader confused	✓ Research is, many times, not put into student's own words ✓ Most of the research/citations come from a single source; a variety of sources is not used ✓ A primary source and direct quotes from it are not used in the paper	✓ Paper has many spelling/grammatical errors, making the paper difficult to read ✓ Paper has inconsistent spacing, style, and size of font, making it difficult to read ✓ Paper has sloppy sentence structures that make paragraphs unclear and difficult to follow

FIGURE 4. Continued.

What Is a Rubric?

A rubric is used to assess mastery for performance-based tasks. Here is a list of various performance assessments (Stanley, 2014):

✓ oral presentations,
✓ debates/speeches,
✓ role playing,
✓ group discussions,
✓ interviews,
✓ portfolios,
✓ exhibitions,
✓ essays,
✓ research papers, and
✓ journals/student logs. (p. 43)

There are two directions you can take when developing a rubric. The rubric can be applied to the assessment, such as the rubric and essay described in Figure 5. The evaluator would have this rubric next to her when going over the work, determining the proper level that best describes the performance of the essay. She might read a

Golden Age Essay Assignment

The period of time in Greek culture known as the "Golden Age" gave many contributions to modern-day society. Describe at least five of these and explain their importance.

A—Students need to choose from the contributions we discussed in class:
- ✓ Democracy
- ✓ Myths
- ✓ Philosophy
- ✓ Historians
- ✓ Olympics
- ✓ Theatre
- ✓ Science
- ✓ Medicine
- ✓ Alphabet
- ✓ Court system

Students need to describe the contribution as the Greeks used it, explaining with detail and examples so that it is clear what the importance was. (Example: Philosophy was contributed by Socrates, Plato, and Aristotle. They taught people to think about ethics and what was right and wrong.)

After describing the contribution, students need to explain how it has contributed to modern-day society, or in other words, how do we use it today. (Example: Myths from Greece are still used in English classes and in children's stories to teach a moral. The story of Narcissus teaches us that we shouldn't be vain.)

This description of the importance and its contribution to modern-day society needs to be clearly explained in all five examples to receive an A.

B—Same as above, but one or two of the choices do not have good examples or clear descriptions of the importance or influence.

C—Choices all came from Greek culture, but three of the choices are not well explained, or all of them are too general without specific detail.

D—One or two of the choices did not come from Greek culture, or there is no explanation of the importance or the influence for most of the choices.

F—Three or more of the choices did not come from Greek culture, or there is no description of the importance or influence. Student may have chosen something from Greek culture that does not have an effect on modern-day society. There may be incorrect information or influences that were not discussed or that come from another culture (e.g., military or bronze, which Greeks did not develop).

FIGURE 5. Sample essay assessment rubric.

response a student has given and apply the B range to it because, although the student mentioned historians, Olympics, medicine, the court system, and democracy, he only explained what the Olympics were, not really explaining their importance to the current world.

You can also reverse this process, taking into account what is provided in the assessment and applying the various levels of the rubric to it. If students were creating a podcast, the rubric might look like Figure 6. While the teacher listens to the podcast, she would determine how to rate it based on the rubric descriptors. If there are just a couple of times when the speakers are hard to hear, the teacher would rate the podcast in the middle tier of the rubric. And if the podcast lasted for 13 minutes, then the teacher would rate the podcast in the top tier. She would try to determine at which levels the assessment fits into the rubric—the end result being a completed rubric that will provide the student with an evaluation.

If a rubric is well written, the teacher should easily be able to match the description with the actions taken in the performance. This is where the subjectivity is taken out of the equation, which is why a well-written rubric is essential for an objective assessment.

What a Rubric Is Not

The major challenge of using a rubric is that it only measures what is written in the rubric. In other words, if there is nothing in the rubric about research skills, and yet the student uses such skills in order to show what she has learned, the evaluator will not be able to rate this specific skill. A rubric is only as good as it is written.

Ideally, you want to give a rubric to students before they begin to work on their performance. This makes the performance expectations clear. Because of this, you cannot add elements to the grading that were not included in the original rubric. For example, you might find that you really should have had something in the rubric about visuals because they are important to the performance, but when making the rubric, you did not include this. You cannot, however, suddenly choose to evaluate visuals because they were not included in the rubric.

Also, the rubric is only as good as the person using it. The evaluator has to understand what the descriptor is asking of the performance. The rubric should be clear in its intent so that the evaluator does not have to make a judgment call, but even a well-written rubric requires that the person using it carefully read through the descriptions and understand what to look for. If an evaluator fails to do this, he or she might not match a student's performance to the correct level of mastery. This is why anchor grading is somewhat important and will be talked about in a later chapter on grading.

Clarity	Content
✓ The podcast can be clearly heard for the entire broadcast, and the participants speak slowly and clearly during the duration. ✓ The information being given is clearly conveyed, and listeners can understand what the podcast is trying to teach them. ✓ The podcast is organized in a manner that makes it easy to follow and understand what is going on at any given time.	✓ Content is explained in detail. ✓ There is obvious research applied to the content, which is used to teach the listener. ✓ Podcast teaches the listener for 10–15 minutes.
✓ The podcast can be clearly heard for most of the broadcast, and the participants speak slowly and clearly during a majority of the duration, but there are a couple of times when it is difficult to hear. ✓ The information being given is clearly conveyed for the most part, and listeners can understand what the podcast is trying to teach them, but there are confusing moments. ✓ The podcast is organized in a manner that makes it easy to follow and understand what is going on at any given time.	✓ Content is explained but lacks detail in places where it is needed. ✓ There is a little research applied to the content, but there needs to be more to clearly teach the listener. ✓ Podcast teaches the listener for 8–9 minutes.
✓ The podcast cannot be heard for a good portion of the broadcast, and/or the participants do not speak slowly and clearly during the duration, making it difficult to understand what they are saying. ✓ The information being given is not clearly conveyed, and listeners have difficulty understanding what the podcast is trying to teach them. ✓ The podcast is not very organized, making it difficult to follow and understand what is going on at any given time.	✓ Content is not well explained, causing confusion. ✓ There is no research applied to the content, failing to teach the reader. ✓ Podcast only teacher for 6 minutes or less.

FIGURE 6. Sample podcast creation rubric.

Assessing This Chapter

Use Reader Assessment 2 (on the following page) to determine your depth of understanding about this chapter.

READER ASSESSMENT 2

On a scale from 1 to 10—1 being you are completely lost and have no idea, and 10 being you have a really good understanding of a concept and could teach others about it—place an X on the following rating scales to indicate your responses to the following five statements:

1. I understand the basic premise of what a rubric is.

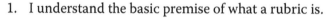

1	5	10

2. I could explain to someone how a rubric is like a blueprint.

1	5	10

3. I clearly understand the difference between a formative and a summative rubric.

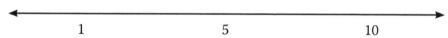

1	5	10

4. With confidence, I could give examples of how a rubric goes into an assessment and how an assessment can go into a rubric.

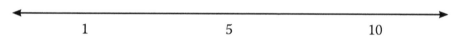

1	5	10

5. I can provide three solid examples of how a rubric can go wrong.

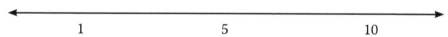

1	5	10

Total Score: _____

- ✓ **40–50:** You have a very good understanding of the material; enjoy the next chapter.
- ✓ **30–39:** You have a good understanding of some of the material but might need to review a section or two.
- ✓ **20–29:** You might want to skim back over the material to see if it triggers any deeper understanding of it.
- ✓ **0–19:** You should definitely reread the chapter, only this time either use a highlighter or take notes to help you remember material.

If your score indicates that you need to go back and reread some parts, this rubric has been a formative one, pointing out gaps in your learning. If your score indicates that you have a good grasp of the chapter, this rubric has been a summative one, acting as an exit ticket before moving on to the next chapter.

Chapter

2

The Advantages
of Rubrics

You may have heard that technology should only be used when it enhances or improves a lesson, not as a replacement for another, equally effective method. Just as with technology, you should not use rubrics for the sake of using rubrics. A rubric should only be used if it is going to properly and objectively evaluate the skills of your students better than another form of assessment. Like most things, there are advantages and disadvantages to using rubrics in the classroom.

Above all, a rubric should properly measure the skill you intend. The best way to ensure this is to make your own rubrics that are tailored to the lessons, students, and teaching style of your classroom, as well as are objective. But why make your own rubric? There are many websites that allow you to plug in a few details and then—voila!—a rubric is generated. Figure 7 is an example of what a website-generated rubric for a class presentation might look like.

There are a few issues with this rubric:

1. Many of the descriptions are vague—"fairly," "somewhat," "good," and "completely." These are all subjective adverbs. If I described someone as "somewhat" smart, this could go in two completely different directions. If one person said, "he is *some*what smart," the inflection could mean the person did not think very highly of his intelligence. However, if he were described as "some*what* smart," the stress seems to indicate that this person is viewed as being bright. The same goes for "fairly." You might think "good" is a description, but it is very subjective as well. What one person considers to be good might be seen differently by someone else. How to make your terminology

Category	4	3	2	1
Posture and Eye Contact	Student stands up straight, looks relaxed and confident, and establishes eye contact with everyone in the room during the presentation.	Student stands up straight and establishes eye contact with everyone in the room during the presentation.	Student sometimes stands up straight and establishes eye contact.	Student slouches and/ or does not make eye contact during the presentation.
Preparedness	Student is completely prepared and has obviously rehearsed.	Student seems fairly prepared but might have needed a couple more rehearsals.	Student is somewhat prepared, but it is clear that rehearsal was lacking.	Student does not seem prepared to present.
Speaks Clearly	Student speaks clearly and distinctly all (i.e., 95%–100%) of the time and does not mispronounce words.	Student speaks clearly and distinctly almost all (i.e., 95%–100%) of the time, but mispronounces one word.	Student speaks clearly and distinctly most (i.e., 85%–94%) of the time, mispronouncing no more than one word.	Student often mumbles or cannot be understood, or mispronounces more than one word.
Content	Student shows a full understanding of the topic.	Student shows a good understanding of the topic.	Student shows a good understanding of parts of the topic.	Student does not seem to understand the topic.

FIGURE 7. Example website-generated rubric.

more specific, and thus easier to identify in a performance, will be discussed in later chapters.

2. This rubric would force the teacher to pay attention to areas that distract from more valuable skills. If the teacher is listening to hear that every word is pronounced correctly, as the rubric describes under "Speaks Clearly," and he or she also has to watch to make sure the speaker makes eye contact with everyone in the room, as described under "Posture and Eye Contact," the teacher might overlook the content being presented. The simpler you

make the rubric, the easier it will be to use. There is a fine balance in having enough description to show the evaluator what to look for, while not having so much description that the evaluator gets lost or confused.

3. The descriptions do not provide specific examples that show the evaluator what to look for. For instance, when the rubric states, "Student is completely prepared," this requires a lot of interpretation. As every English teacher tells students, show—don't tell. A way to show would be, "Student brings all of her materials and makes smooth and clear transitions that help with listeners' understanding of the topic." The evaluator can see that and now knows what to look for. The "Posture and Eye Contact" category does a better job of showing the evaluator what to look for than some of the other categories. The more specific you are with showing, the easier the rubric is for an evaluator to use and understand.

4. The rubric would allow other aspects to inflate students' grades rather than actually show their mastery—everything seems to be equally weighted. If you speak clearly you could get upwards to a 4, and the same goes if you have a full understanding of the topic. However, are those two equal in importance? That would, of course, depend on what the learning target for the lesson was. If the learning target had to do with content, that would seem to be more important. However, if the teacher is evaluating 21st-century skills, such as public speaking, then that might be the important aspect. Whichever is most important, however, is going to be inflated by the other categories. For example, let us say the learning target has to do with content. If the student nails the posture, preparedness, and speaking clearly, she is going to get high marks overall, even if she does not know her content very well. The grade reflects a B on the learning target, when in actuality it was a D. Thus, the rubric does not measure what the teacher has determined to be important for the lesson. The rubric needs to be able to accurately measure the level of mastery of the student.

5. The rubric is too specific with some of the language—when it says, "Student speaks clearly and distinctly all (i.e., 95%–100%) of the time," it would be difficult to determine what that actually looks like. How is the evaluator supposed to evaluate what is 94% of the time, which is the next level down? You want to be specific in your descriptions, but not so specific that your descriptions make the performance difficult to measure. This is clearly a case of telling, not showing.

This example rubric is subjective and lacks validity. Using this rubric to measure a student's mastery of a lesson would be like using a sundial to record someone's running time. It may give you a general idea, but it is just not going to be very accurate. That is the single greatest advantage to creating your own rubrics; they can be tailored to what you are measuring and accurately convey the level of mastery.

There are other advantages to making your own rubrics. First, you know your lesson well; after all, you are the one who created or adapted it. By making your own rubric, you can customize it to fit your lesson like a proverbial glove. Watching a teacher print a rubric that he or she found online and try to make it fit with a lesson is always painful. The online rubric may measure some of what the teacher intends to assess, but it will also miss some skills or measure skills that were of less importance. You want a rubric to be a lean machine, with no excess fat or unwanted parts. You know best what you want to measure. By writing a rubric yourself, you can ensure your intent is captured properly.

Second, you know your students well. This means that you know how to set expectations as well. If you have a class with many high-achieving students, you might want to shape the rubric to challenge them. If, on the other hand, you have a lot of students who struggle, you can scaffold the rubric to match their abilities. You might teach five of the same classes but determine you need a couple of different rubrics to meet the specific needs of your students.

Third, you know your grading style. As teachers, we are all looking for different things. One science teacher might not focus heavily on spelling and grammar when it comes to student written work, while another might think them of great importance. There are a lot of things that are standard in our educational system, such as content standards, state tests, and curriculum. One of the few unique things is the teaching style and expectations of individual teachers. By creating your own rubrics, you can capture these expectations and make clear to students what you value as a teacher.

The Assessment of Survival Skills

One of the biggest advantages to creating a rubric is that you are able to measure mastery for skills that are more difficult to translate to the gradebook. In other words, a rubric can measure things that other instruments are unable to. Traditional assessments can usually only assess knowledge in the form of content or the application of said content. Rubrics, on the other hand, can evaluate processes and products.

Processes are the physical manipulation of skills. When taking a pencil-to-paper test, the act of writing is a process. You could evaluate handwriting, spelling and grammar, and organization. These are all demonstrations of skills. Another example would be playing a musical instrument. This is a demonstration of a student's ability to play the instrument. You cannot show this ability on a traditional, multiple-choice test. The only way you can display this ability is through performance. This is where a rubric comes into play. It can capture the performance and break it down. One could listen to the student playing the musical instrument and think that he or she did an overall good job playing it. Figure 8 is an example of a rubric to evaluate musical performances.

The rubric takes the overall musical performance and breaks it down into three categories; rhythm, melody, and expressiveness. In its descriptions of each of these, the rubric clearly shows what each aspect looks like. Under "Melody," the superior description is "Can play a new melodic phrase without any help from instructor." If you are not a music teacher, you may not know what this sounds like, but someone with some musical background would know exactly what to listen for. By breaking down the overall performance, this rubric delves into the processes used in the musical performance of the student.

Rubrics can be used to capture processes, such as:
- ✓ physical skills (e.g., the ability to throw a ball or correctly perform CPR);
- ✓ proper use of equipment (e.g., knowing how a microscope works, using a tool to make something in woodshop);
- ✓ work and study habits (e.g., having a system to take notes, being able to work as part of a group);
- ✓ public speaking (e.g., giving a presentation or giving a performance, such as a skit or debate); or
- ✓ task-based skills (e.g., being able to properly read aloud, demonstrating you know how to tie your shoe).

Rubrics can also objectively evaluate products. Products are usually the end result of a lesson or task in which one is asked to produce something that demonstrates mastery has been attained. Some examples of products might include:
- ✓ objects that are physically constructed (e.g., a model of a volcano or a wooden bookshelf);
- ✓ a summative representation of what was learned (e.g., a portfolio or an exhibition piece);
- ✓ written products (e.g., essays, research papers, or lab reports);
- ✓ technology (e.g., a website, a podcast, or a PowerPoint); or
- ✓ ideas (e.g., a manifesto or a poem).

Figure 9 is an example of a holistic rubric for evaluating a product. This is rather simple; the student either showed mastery of the skill or did not. The evaluator reads the descriptor and determines how to rate the student's performance.

	Developing	Standard	Above Standard	Expert
Rhythm	Cannot play complex sheet music while matching metronome speed	Can sometimes play complex sheet music while matching metronome speed, but inconsistently	Most times able to play sheet music while matching metronome speed	Consistently able to play sheet music patterns while matching metronome speed
Melody	Cannot play a new melodic phrase, or can but with constant help from instructor	Can play a new melodic phrase, but needs a lot of help from instructor	Can play a new melodic phrase, but needs a little help from instructor	Can play a new melodic phrase without any help from instructor
Expressiveness	Inconsistently meets the requirements of the music	Meets the requirements of the music but not with sensitivity	Most times meets the requirements of the music with sensitivity	Responds to requirements of the music with nuances and sensitivity

FIGURE 8. Rubric for scoring music performance evaluation for grades K–12. Adapted from Ohio Department of Education, 2009.

Other Advantages of Rubrics

Rubrics are an effective tool for evaluating authentic experiences. This is because authentic experiences are rarely ever a multiple-choice test or a worksheet. Authentic experiences involve actually doing something in the real world.

Figure 10 is an example of a rubric used to evaluate an authentic community service project. It would be challenging to try to determine mastery for an authentic project like this using another instrument, but a rubric allows the teacher to evaluate the actions of the student and determine whether he met the requirements of this authentic task. Not only is this rubric able to evaluate the service project itself, but it also measures the responsibility of the student. Responsibility is an authentic skill that every teacher should promote in the classroom, but because it is hard to measure, it does not get enough focus. Instead, many classrooms hold the responsibility of inauthentic tasks, such as turning in homework, bringing books to class, or behaving in class, over the heads of students. Which scenario do you think would be more empowering and thus authentic to students?

Impressionist Art Evaluator Grading Rubric

Art Example(s): For passing

Student has color examples of art works that can be easily viewed by all:
- ✓ Japonisme: A woodcut and early Impressionist art painting in color for comparison.
- ✓ Early Impressionist: Two works of art in color by artist(s) of the period.
- ✓ Impressionist Poetry: Compares characteristics of Romantic poetry with Impressionist poetry.
- ✓ Music: Shows common theme between Impressionist poetry and music. A selection of music must be played.
- ✓ African Masks: Compares an African mask with an example of an Early Modern/ Post-Impressionist work of art showing an obvious influence.
- ✓ Post-Impressionist: At least one work of art, in color, which characterizes a specific Early Modern/Post-Impressionist movement.

Student Art: For passing

This grade is based on effort and the explanation of how an important aspect of the student's research relates to the medium selected. The work of art does not have to be in the same style as the report. For example, a student doing a report on Impressionist Music may have created an African mask. Student also has an option to create a work of art or attempt an interpretation of the Impressionist or Post-Impressionist style.

Art Example(s): For not passing

Student has an example of a work of art, which cannot be easily seen by all. (Does not meet the criteria for an "A." Student has some difficulty explaining why the work relates to the topic.)

Student Art: For not passing

The student's work shows little effort, and the explanation of how and/or why it relates to the project is weak.

FIGURE 9. Example holistic rubric.

Rubrics help clarify what teachers' expectations are for students. Different teachers hold different expectations for students. What one teacher would give a student an A on in his class, another teacher might award a C for in hers. A student might have a social studies teacher who believes strongly in learning dates and key terms, while another might care more about understanding trends and broader changes over time. Students may spend the better part of a school year trying to determine what a teacher's expectations are and then trying to meet them. Rubrics

Community Service Project

Overall	Service Project	Responsibility
Excellent	✓ Student has multiple pieces of evidence of his or her project in the form of photos, letters from those helped, and/or video of the service project. ✓ Student conducts a service project with long-term results, rather than something that is short-term and surface level. ✓ Student is able to meaningfully convey how his or her project helped the community and the value of such an action.	✓ Student completes the service project when he or she is supposed to according to the calendar created, and works additionally on the project, extending it beyond the assignment. ✓ Student stays on task throughout the project, showing specific evidence of this whenever conferencing with the teacher. ✓ Student was able to act independently on the project without intervention from the teacher.
Good	✓ Student has evidence of his or her project but only in a single form of photos, letters from those helped, or video of the service project. ✓ Student conducts a successful service project, but the results are short-term and at a surface level. ✓ Student is able to convey how his or her project helped the community and the value of such an action at a surface level, but without much meaning.	✓ Student completes the service project when he or she is supposed to according to the calendar created. ✓ Student stays mostly on task throughout the project, occasionally getting a little off, but still showing specific evidence whenever conferencing with the teacher. ✓ Student was mostly able to act independently on the project, but occasionally needed intervention from the teacher.
Needs Improvement	✓ Student does not have concrete evidence of his or her project, only anecdotal evidence that cannot be backed up. ✓ Student does not conduct a successful service project, letting obstacles and roadblocks stop him or her from moving forward. ✓ Student is not able to convey how his or her project helped the community or the value of such an action.	✓ Student needs more time than the calendar allows to complete the service project. ✓ Student does not stay on task throughout the project, or cannot provide any specific evidence to show this whenever conferencing with the teacher. ✓ Student was not able to act independently on the project, needing much intervention from the teacher.

FIGURE 10. Example community service project rubric. Adapted from *10 Performance-Based STEM Projects for grades 6–8* (p. 59), by T. Stanley, 2018, Waco, New York, NY: Routledge Copyright 2018 by Taylor & Francis. Adapted with permission.

make expectations more transparent. Students can clearly see what is important to the teacher because it is included in the rubric.

Rubrics also clearly show how work will be evaluated. Think of the numerous times that students have complained about not knowing that the teacher was going to be grading for something. A rubric does not allow for excuses. A rubric's language and wording make it clear how the work is to be evaluated. Students can use a rubric as a blueprint to make sure they are following expectations and are graded on what the teacher detailed for them in the rubric.

Rubrics provide easy access to differentiated instruction. Teachers have all sorts of levels of students in their classrooms. Advanced students need to be challenged more, while struggling students might need more scaffolding to succeed. Rubrics are naturally scaffolded. Because there are different levels of performance, if you have a class with a wide spectrum of student ability, you could use the rubric as a way to differentiate. Figure 11 is an example.

Notice with this rubric that the mastery level has been set in the middle tier. This gives students who are more advanced the opportunity to improve and build upon the assignment even further, while those who may still be developing can still work toward meeting the core expectations.

Additional Advantages for Students

Using rubrics can keep students focused during an assessment. How many times has the following happened? You start out a lesson with the best of intentions, asking that students create a really cool product that will help them to learn the focus of the lesson, only for some of them to get so caught up in the product that they neglect what they were supposed to learn. For example, if students were learning about perimeter and area by designing and creating a fort, a student might turn in a beautiful model made of popsicle sticks, with a swimming pool, fireman's pole, and a trampoline room. When you ask the student what the perimeter of the fort is, he looks at you with confusion and says, "Perimeter?"

To avoid this scenario, provide students with the rubric at the beginning of the lesson or project. Then, remind students to refer to the rubric throughout the process. As stated before, a rubric is the blueprint for success, telling students exactly what they need to do in order to achieve mastery. Before a student turns in the end product, she should use the rubric to determine if there is anything missing or that needs to be improved in her work. This constant checking in with the rubric ensures that nothing is overlooked and that the focus of the lesson remains front and center.

By using rubrics regularly in your classroom, students will begin to develop a common vocabulary. This is because you will use terms and measurements that stu-

Notes Rubric			
Overall	**Organization**	**Readability**	**Content**
Above and Beyond	✓ Notes are easy to follow, appearing on one side of the page and starting a new page when another topic begins ✓ Student uses headings consistently so that topic shifts are easy to see; there are additional headings to help one locate important information ✓ Notes are in order and complete, providing an organizational key to easily find main points	✓ Handwriting is legible; everything is readable ✓ Notes are spaced out; readers can tell where one piece of information ends and another begins; note-taking strategies discussed in class are clearly used ✓ System of shorthand allows the reader to clearly tell what is written, and there is a key for easy translation	✓ Student has a deeper grasp of the content than the presentation provided, giving a good understanding of the various aspects of the topic ✓ Student includes important information that was emphasized in the lecture, marking the information as significant ✓ Key definitions are written out clearly and somehow set apart from the other notes to make them easier to find
Mastered	✓ Notes are easy to follow with a clear pattern to each section ✓ Student uses headings consistently so that topic shifts are easy to see ✓ Notes are in order and complete	✓ Handwriting is legible; almost everything is readable ✓ Notes are spaced out; readers can tell where one piece of information ends and another begins ✓ System of shorthand allows the reader to clearly tell what is written	✓ Student includes enough content, providing a good understanding of the various aspects of the topic ✓ Student includes important information that was emphasized in the lecture, marking the information as significant ✓ Key definitions are written out clearly

FIGURE 11. Example rubric scaffolding for differentiation.

Overall	Organization	Readability	Content
Still Needs Work	✓ Notes can be followed for the most part with a pattern to each section, but they occasionally skip around ✓ Student uses headings so that topic shifts are easy to see, but not always consistently ✓ Notes are in order and complete most of the time, but not always	✓ Handwriting is legible for the most part, but there are sections that are difficult to read ✓ Notes are spaced out for the most part, but readers cannot always tell where one piece of information ends and another begins ✓ System of shorthand allows the reader to tell what is written, but not always	✓ Student includes content, providing a good understanding of most of the various aspects of the topic ✓ Student includes most of the important information that was emphasized in the lecture, but doesn't always mark it as significant ✓ Key definitions are included, but not always written clearly

FIGURE 11. Continued.

dents will come to understand as they see them repeated again and again. Definitions of certain vocabulary, such as "accurate," "detail," or "professional," can vary. Making sure students know your definition of terms such as these is important, as is being consistent in their use in order for students to be successful. It is even more ideal to have vertical alignment between grades. What if the eighth-, ninth-, and 10th-grade English language arts (ELA) classes all used a similar rubric with consistent vocabulary, adding more rigor in each grade level? This way, when a student walks into his 10th-grade ELA class and sees the rubric, he knows exactly how to define the terms because he has seen them many times.

Once students get used to the fact that you are using rubrics regularly in your classroom, they will begin to use them to self-evaluate. You, of course, can help at first with this, giving students a practice day to work on a performance and having classmates evaluate each other using the rubric and discussing the results. After doing this for a while, students will likely form a habit of using rubric criteria to self-evaluate. How many times have you seen a student get up to do a presentation and, after the first 20 seconds, it becomes painfully obvious that it is the first time the student is giving the presentation? Students need to learn that, just as you do not turn in a first draft of a paper because there will be many mistakes, you do not give the first draft of a performance. Similarly, a student might use the rubric to check over a research paper or essay. Getting students into the habit of using the rubric to improve their performance is a valuable skill for them to learn, as it will mean their work will be that much better.

Asking students to create a rubric can also act as a motivational tool. Chapter 7 goes into much more detail about student-created rubrics, but to summarize, students are much more involved in a lesson when they feel that they have had some input into its creation. Student buy in can increase dramatically if you allow them to be part of the process in creating the lesson rubric rather than just handing them a sheet of paper. Any time you engage students by giving them choice and making them part of the learning process can make a lesson more valuable and effective.

A lot of times, students complete work and then wait for the teacher to determine how they did. What if students could determine this for themselves? Rubrics can be used to teach students to track their own growth, making them self-reflective learners. They could have the rubric ahead of time and then be able to take their work and progress and assess their level of understanding and mastery. Imagine if students came to the conclusion of how well they are learning by themselves. How empowering would that be? This could be done over the course of a school year so that students are able to determine for themselves how much learning they have accomplished. This would enable students to become self-reflective and, more importantly, learn for themselves.

Assessing This Chapter

This chapter discussed the many advantages of creating your own rubrics. Use Reader Assessment 3 (on the following page) to determine how important you feel each of the following advantages are for teachers.

READER ASSESSMENT 3

Advantage to Teacher	Not All That Valuable	Pretty Valuable	Extremely Valuable
Rubrics remove the personal part of grading—sometimes it can be a challenge to take out the personal bias of grading, whether this is explicit or implicit. You might have a student who worked really hard but did not meet the criteria needed, or there might be that student who you feel messed around in class only to pull it together for the performance. An objective rubric takes this bias out of the equation and evaluates the student only on his or her performance.			
Rubrics help coordinate instruction and assessment—ideally, a rubric should be designed for repeated use, over time, on several tasks. Students are given a rubric at the beginning of a lesson. They do the work, receive feedback, practice, revise or do another task, continue to practice, and then, usually, are given a grade using the same rubric. This method of assessment is much more consistent than a variety of assignments with related but different ways to evaluate.			
Rubrics allow for different types of assessments—grading multiple-choice tests or worksheets in which the answers are all the same can be very tedious, especially if you have hundreds of papers to grade. Using rubrics allows the teacher to offer open-ended assignments that provide the teacher with a variety of solutions and thought-provoking responses.			
Rubrics help teachers teach—if you have made a good rubric, instead of constantly having to remind students of the expectations or point out what the focus of the lesson is, you can simply refer them to the rubric. This starts to take the responsibility out the hands of the teacher, and puts it firmly in the lap of the student.			
Rubrics will make you more aware of the "why" in grading—you want to be clear about why you are evaluating the student the way you are, and rubrics provide these criteria. Rubrics make you more aware of this "why" so that you are grading in an objective manner rather than just because of a feeling. Oftentimes, these feelings can be correct about a student work, but the rubric just clarifies and justifies these feelings.			

Chapter

3

Types of Rubrics

There is no one type of rubric to use for every situation. Just like tools in a toolbox, you do not pull out the hammer for every job you have. If you have to saw something in half, a hammer is going to be a crude tool at best. You want to make sure you have the best tool for the job. This requires matching the right rubric to the right assessment.

General Versus Task-Specific Descriptions

A rubric is made up of descriptions that show what each level of evaluation looks like. When setting levels of evaluation, you have to decide how specific the rubric's descriptions will be. A description for evaluating a research paper might read, "Paper is written coherently and is easy to follow." This description of the paper gives characteristics that apply to a series of tasks that must occur in order for the student to arrive at this point.

A general description can help students see the big picture. In life, we are often rewarded not for the small details, but rather the finished product. For example, if someone makes a pizza, they are complimented on the finished product. "Wow, that pizza was delicious." Someone is not going to go into great detail by specifically describing various aspects of that pizza. This general description is adequate to establish a range of performance. Either he loved that pizza, he liked it, or he did not like it. Helping students see the larger picture and that good work is bigger than one task goes a long way in preparing them for the real world.

Rubrics with general descriptions are also practical. If a language arts teacher writes a general rubric for how essays should be evaluated, the teacher can use this every time he assigns an essay. More than that, because students have seen the rubric before, they become familiar with the expectations for what they need to do to be successful. Of course, the disadvantage of a general rubric is in the name itself. Because of its generality, sometimes a general rubric does not allow the teacher to get specific enough with students. They may know overall that their mechanics were not up to par, but students may not know that capitalization errors were the specific issue. The feedback from a general rubric may not be specific enough.

Task-specific rubrics, on the other hand, provide this specificity. Their advantage is that they break down tasks to the point that students and the teacher can easily see what the strengths and weaknesses are and then can make adjustments. Because of this, task-specific rubrics tend to be a more reliable assessment of student performance. You get a truer picture of what a student is and is not capable of. Using the example from before, a general rubric would simply say, "This pizza is delicious," "This pizza is OK," or "This pizza is lousy." A task-specific rubric would break the task of making the pizza into more criteria, such as:

✓ kneading the dough;
✓ adding oregano and other spices in tomato paste to create the sauce;
✓ grating the cheese;
✓ putting on additional ingredients, such as pepperoni, sausage, and/or mushrooms;
✓ preheating the oven to 375°; and
✓ cooking for 18 to 20 minutes.

The advantage of being more task-specific is that if something goes wrong with the end product, the cause of the problem can more easily be pinpointed. Maybe the student heated the oven to 475° and the pizza was overcooked, or oregano was not added and the pizza tasted rather bland. Errors like this can then be corrected for the next time, which will hopefully lead to better success. The devil is, indeed, sometimes in the details.

Because task-specific rubrics break evaluation criteria down into more detail, they can make the evaluation much clearer to the evaluator. A teacher does not have to discern what a rubric means when it says, "Presentation is very creative," and instead can assess a student's work using more precise descriptions, such as:

✓ "Student uses self-created visual aids that add to the viewer's understanding,"
✓ "Student approaches the problem from a unique point of view," or
✓ "Presentation is given in an engaging manner; presentation involves the audience members or excites them."

These more specific criteria describe what teachers should look for and give them guidance. Task-specific rubrics, however, can also be a disadvantage if the descriptors do not show certain aspects that appear in the student work. How does the teacher evaluate if something is not specifically shown? A general rubric would give a teacher more wiggle room to interpret what a criterion looks like rather than having it prescribed.

The biggest disadvantage to creating task-specific rubrics is that all-important aspect of time. If a rubric is task-specific, it probably cannot be used for other assignments. There might be elements that can be reused, but, for the most part, the rubric would have to be rewritten for each lesson. This can be time consuming. The ultimate question the teacher has to ask is whether this time is worth it, considering the additional details and information that he will receive about his students.

Holistic Versus Analytic Rubrics

One you have decided whether you are going to utilize general or task-specific descriptions, you need to decide on the type of rubric. There are two basic schools of thought—holistic rubrics and analytical rubrics.

Holistic Rubrics

Just as its name suggests, a holistic rubric looks at the whole picture. If a student is completing a performance assessment, such as an essay, the evaluator would look at all aspects of the written piece and narrow all of the criteria into a single grade. The rubric might look like Figure 12.

For each level in this holistic rubric, there is a series of descriptors that show what that level looks like. The evaluator decides where this particular student's performance fits in. Each level scaffolds down as the grades get lower. You can see this in the grammatical errors descriptor, in which errors cause no distractions at the A level, are slightly distracting at the B level, include some misspellings at the C level, and include many misspellings and grammatical errors at the D–F level. Using this rubric, the evaluator would look at the entirety of the student's performance in order to gauge how the work aligns with the rubric. The student may have met some criteria and may be missing others, but the evaluator will have to make the best match based on the four grade-level categories provided.

There are advantages and disadvantages to holistic rubrics. One advantage is that evaluators can score faster. Because criteria are grouped into level categories, a teacher can more easily evaluate hard-to-score performances. A holistic rubric min-

---

A—Exceeds expectations: The reader is able to easily identify the essay's focus and is engaged by its clear examples and relevant details. Information is presented in a very organized manner. Grammatical errors or misspelled words do not distract the reader.

B—Above average: The reader is easily able to identify the essay's focus, and the essay is supported by relevant examples and supporting details. Information is presented in an organized manner that makes the essay easy to follow. Misspellings and/or grammatical errors distract the reader slightly from the flow of the paper.

C—Average: The reader can identify the essay's focus without much difficulty, and supporting examples are present and clear. The information is presented in an organized manner that can be followed with little difficulty. There are some misspellings and/or grammatical errors, but they do not seriously distract from the work.

D–F—Below average: The reader cannot clearly or easily identify the focus of the essay. Information is disorganized, making the essay difficult to follow. There are many misspellings and/or grammatical errors that interfere with the reader's ability to follow the essay.

FIGURE 12. Example holistic essay rubric.

---

imizes the number of decisions an evaluator has to make, which allows him or her to pay more attention to a student's performance. An example would be a debate. A teacher must watch the performances while taking notes and trying to determine how the performance aligns with the rubric. If there are a lot of things to consider on the rubric, the evaluator might be busy reviewing the rubric or recording student results while something important is occurring in the debate. Depending on the performance you are evaluating, a holistic rubric might be better to capture subjective criteria more accurately and with more consistency. For example, if a student is being evaluated on a formal presentation, there are a lot of things to look for, such as posture, volume, content, lack of "ums" and "ahs"—the list can go on and on. However, if the holistic rubric were to read, "Student gives a professional looking and sounding presentation," then the performance will be much easier for the rater to evaluate while it is underway. Instead of looking at numerous things separately, the rater is looking at the performance holistically, or what the summation of all of the parts looks like in the finished product.

A holistic rubric is better suited as a summative, rather than formative, assessment because it focuses typically on what the learner can do, not what he cannot. This leads to one of its disadvantages, which is that it does not provide much detail on what was done well and what was done poorly because all of the learning objectives are grouped together at each level of performance. A holistic rubric is great for assessing a single dimension, but if you are looking for students to meet multiple objectives, an analytical rubric might be more useful.

Analytical Rubrics

An analytical rubric analyzes student performance, breaking it down into smaller parts or characteristics. An analytical rubric allows the evaluator to show the exact areas in which students display strengths and areas in which students display need for improvement. If we revise the holistic rubric from Figure 12, we can break it down into three different parts (see Figure 13), giving the evaluator a chance to look at criteria more individually.

You will notice that the analytical rubric includes almost the same criteria as the holistic rubric. Now, however, the evaluator can make clear to the student which specific aspects of the essay went well and which ones could be improved. Using this rubric, the scorer would be able to mark down for grammar and yet high for content, giving a better picture of what skills the student needs to improve. The student also has a clearer idea of why she received the grade she did. Nothing is more wasteful for a student than to get a grade and not know the reasons for it. How does one expect to get better or to repeat good skills if she does not know what they are, what they look like, how she used them, and when she used them?

Analytical rubrics provide formative feedback to both the student and the teacher. If a student writes a rough draft of the essay and the teacher uses a rubric to evaluate it, the student might learn that, although he scored an A on grammar and spelling and a B on content, his organization was very poor, resulting in a D. Now he can address this in his final draft, fixing the problems with organization. Also, because the skills are broken down, the rubric makes it is easier for the teacher to link the skills to instruction. Using the example from before, a teacher could put three individual grades in the gradebook. Maybe one of these, like grammar and spelling, is not an objective for the lesson but is something the teacher feels she should be teaching throughout the year, while the content aspect might link more closely to the specific learning objective. The teacher can apply the content grade to that specific lesson but record the grammar and spelling grade as overall progress of the student.

In an analytical rubric, you have to not only describe what the actions look like when the student does them right, but also show what they look like when they are done incorrectly. This, of course, takes time—time to create the rubric and more time to evaluate the performance. And, oftentimes, providing a lot of detail as to why the student got the grade she did does not mean she is going to read the rubric. There has been many a student who glanced at the letter grade on the rubric and then either pitched the rubric into the trash can or left it behind when the bell rang. Chapter 8 describes in more detail how to effectively return a rubric to a student and provide feedback so that he or she understands the grade. Another disadvantage of analytical rubrics is that if the descriptors are unclear, because there are so many additional aspects to evaluate, rater reliability will be more difficult to attain.

	Content	Organization	Grammar/Spelling
A	The reader is able to easily identify the essay's focus and is engaged by the essay's clear examples and relevant details.	Information is presented in a very organized manner.	Grammatical errors or misspelled words do not distract the reader.
B	The reader is easily able to identify the essay's focus, and the essay is supported by relevant examples and supporting details.	Information is presented in an organized manner that is easy to follow.	Misspellings and/or grammatical errors distract the reader slightly from the flow of the paper.
C	The reader can identify the essay's focus without much difficulty, and supporting examples are present and clear.	The information is presented in an organized manner that can be followed with little difficulty.	There are some misspellings and/or grammatical errors, but they do not seriously distract from the work.
D–F	The reader cannot clearly or easily identify the essay's focus.	Information is not very organized, making the essay difficult to follow.	There are many misspellings and/or grammatical errors that interfere with the reader's ability to follow the essay.
	Score:	Score:	Score:

FIGURE 13. Example analytical essay rubric.

One person could use the rubric and grade the assignment one way, while another scorer might end up with different grade. Chapter 8 also shows you how to anchor grade to ensure that a rubric is more objective and that the scores are more consistent amongst evaluators.

Developmental rubrics. The developmental rubric is a version of the analytic rubric, but its sole purpose is to evaluate progress, not an end product. You would not convert a developmental rubric into a summative rubric. A developmental rubric is purely formative. Every developmental rubric should ask the same essential question, which is "How well are students developing the skill?" A developmental rubric serves as a roadmap to determine where your students have gone, where they are, and where they are going. The rubric should cover an extended period of time, perhaps even months, rather than a single activity. If done correctly, a developmental rubric will assess students on a continuum that shows the long-term progress of their development.

	Above Average	Average	Below Average
Throwing a Ball	Throws both accurately and with control	Throws accurately or with control, but not both	Throws wildly or without control
Walking a Beam	Walks both forward and backward along the beam without falling	Walks forward on the beam without falling	Walks along the beam with assistance
Kicking at a Target	Kicks with accuracy consistently	Kicks with accuracy, but inconsistently	Consistently does not kick with accuracy
Date of observation:	Notes:	Notes:	Notes:

FIGURE 14. Example developmental rubric for athletic activities.

Figure 14 is a rubric that a physical education teacher could use to track the developmental progress of students in regard to specific athletic activities. This teacher could complete one of these rubrics each week, creating a running portfolio for a student that describes his development. The teacher could then review these developmental rubrics to see if the student is progressing. There might even be a time when the student exceeds the expectations and an additional rubric would need to be created to chart his course.

Single-point rubrics. Another derivative of the analytical rubric, a single-point rubric breaks down a lesson into specific criteria but only describes the criteria for basic mastery, leaving out the ways a student could go above and beyond or display deficiencies, and instead allowing the criteria to be more open-ended. A single-point rubric might look like Figure 15. This rubric shows the students only what mastery looks like. Anything above or below is left wide open for the teacher to provide notes to steer students to improve or to praise them for work that is exceptional.

Single-point rubrics take much less time to create than other types, and because they are simpler, students are more likely to actually look at them. The teacher does not also have to predict ways students can go wrong or exceed expectations ahead of time. A single-point rubric actually removes the ceiling on learning, allowing a student to stretch as far as he or she can. The teacher can simply respond to examples of what she sees, making comments in the space provided. A single-point does require the teacher to write more when assessing. Instead of simply circling the proper level of achievement if a student has struggled with a lesson, the teacher will have to take more time to write his or her comments.

Concerns	Graphs/Tables	Advanced
	✓ Graphs are clearly labeled; the viewer can easily understand the information being conveyed. ✓ Graphs are professional-looking and organize the predicted weather against the actual weather in a way that is easy to compare and see the differences/similarities.	
Concerns	**Portfolio**	**Advanced**
	✓ Portfolio is well-organized, with all sections flowing into one another, and is easy to follow. ✓ Seven well-developed sections are included. ✓ Written sections use lots of detail and examples to illustrate the points being made.	
Concerns	**Content**	**Advanced**
	✓ Describes the typical weather in the season, why that weather occurs, and how the observed weather compares in detail and with evidence. ✓ Conclusion compares the results versus the predictions and analyzes them using data from the graphs/tables. ✓ Reflection is thoughtful and shares the feelings of the students with much detail.	

FIGURE 15. Example single-point rubric. Adapted from *10 Performance-Based STEM Projects for grades 2–3* (p. 94), by T. Stanley, 2018, Waco, New York, NY: Routledge Copyright 2018 by Taylor & Francis. Adapted with permission.

Assessing This Chapter

Use Reader Assessment 4 (on the following page) to determine your progress so far.

READER ASSESSMENT 4

Before You Started This Book	Feel Very Confident	Feel Somewhat Confident	Some Confidence but Could Use More	Little to No Confidence
If colleagues were having a discussion about rubrics, I would have no trouble joining in.				
If a colleague asked me for a suggestion for what sort of rubric she should use, I would be able to give her an example.				
If a colleague asked me to help her create a rubric, I would have a good idea of what to do.				

At This Point in the Book	Feel Very Confident	Feel Somewhat Confident	Some Confidence but Could Use More	Little to No Confidence
If colleagues were having a discussion about rubrics, I would have no trouble joining in.				
If a colleague asked me for a suggestion for what sort of rubric she should use, I would be able to give her an example.				
If a colleague asked me to help her create a rubric, I would have a good idea of what to do.				

After Finishing the Book	Feel Very Confident	Feel Somewhat Confident	Some Confidence but Could Use More	Little to No Confidence
If colleagues were having a discussion about rubrics, I would have no trouble joining in.				
If a colleague asked me for a suggestion for what sort of rubric she should use, I would be able to give her an example.				
If a colleague asked me to help her create a rubric, I would have a good idea of what to do.				

Chapter

4

Creating Reliable and Valid Assessments

Rubrics are only as good as the person creating them. Because there are so many bad rubrics out there that do not properly measure students' mastery, there are many educators who feel rubrics cannot be as objective as a multiple-choice test. That, however, is incorrect. Rubrics can be just as, if not more, objective than a multiple-choice test. You just need to make sure that they are both reliable and valid.

Reliability

Understanding reliability and validity ensures that a rubric is created with these two important aspects in mind. First, we must define what these terms mean. *Reliability* is defined as

> the extent to which a questionnaire, test, observation or any measurement procedure produces the same results on repeated trials. In short, it is the stability or consistency of scores over time or across raters. Keep in mind that reliability pertains to *scores* not people. Thus, in research we would never say that someone was reliable. As an example, consider judges in a platform diving competition. The

extent to which they agree on the scores for each contestant is an indication of reliability. Similarly, the degree to which an individual's responses (i.e., their scores) on a survey would stay the same over time is also a sign of reliability. An important point to understand is that a measure can be perfectly reliable and yet not be valid. (Miller, 2007, p. 1)

In short, when an assessment is reliable, it will give you replicable results. A good way to test this with a rubric is to ask three people to assess the same performance using the rubric. If the results span a wide range of scores, the rubric's reliability may be in question. There may be too much room for interpretation in the descriptors, resulting in the evaluators arriving at different conclusions. The descriptors probably need to be more detailed and show the evaluators what the performance looks like, so that they do not have to imagine it. Reliability is also the ability to use a rubric once with a student and use it again with that student and see a similar result.

Figure 16 is a snippet from an example of an unreliable rubric. Consider a student giving a presentation on photosynthesis, adhering to these descriptors, making sure to speak clearly and at a good volume, while being organized to the point that he is easy to follow. The teacher indicates that the student was in the top range and assigns the student an A. Another student gives a similar performance on her presentation, seemingly speaking with the same consistency and at the same volume, following the same basic outline that the other student did. The teacher, however, rates this student's performance in a lower range (see Figure 17). What are the students to think, especially the second one? She gave a similar performance and yet received a different result. If a rubric is reliable, it will award the same grade for the same level of performance.

Validity

Validity is whether an assessment measures what you intend it to measure. After all, if a rubric does not assess what it intends to, there will be serious problems with the objectivity in scoring. A rubric should be valid because the assumptions by the student and parent are that if the child was graded for something, then that grade truly reflects the student's mastery level for that particular skill. Consider, for example, a student whose work is rated as "superior" on an essay assignment about understanding the differences between physical and chemical changes. Yet, when the report card comes out, the student has received a C for his particular learning objective. When the parents ask the teacher about this at conferences, the teacher

---

Presentation

✓ Speaker presents clearly consistently throughout; does not read to audience
✓ Student speaks at a reasonable volume that can be heard by all, but is not obnoxious
✓ Presentation is organized in a professional manner, making it easy to follow what is being discussed at any given time

---

FIGURE 16. Example top range of an unreliable rubric.

Presentation

✓ Speaker presents clearly most times; reads to audience only occasionally
✓ Student speaks at a reasonable volume for most of the presentation, but he or she is difficult to hear a few times
✓ Presentation is organized, making it easy to follow what is being discussed, but it is not as professional as it could be

---

FIGURE 17. Example lower range of an unreliable rubric.

---

says that the student has a decent general understanding of the differences between physical and chemical changes, but not a deep understanding of the concept. The question then becomes: Why was the student evaluated as "superior"? The answer, of course, is that the rubric did not properly measure the depth of understanding.

There are three factors that determine whether a rubric is valid. These factors are the three C's—content, criterion, and construct. *Content validity* is whether the combined parts of the rubric add up to the whole picture of the skill being evaluated. For example, if you have a rubric that is supposed to measure a student's ability to write clearly and you have broken that aspect of the rubric into three parts—sentence structure, mechanics, and organization—you cannot determine, just because the student's mechanics are good, that this student knows how to write clearly. You would need to evaluate multiple factors that go into clear writing to determine whether a student has mastered that skill or not.

Criterion validity is how the rubric measures a skill. If you have a rubric that is supposed to measure a student's ability to follow and understand the Pythagorean theorem and the student does not demonstrate this ability, although the rubric indicates that she did, that is a problem. The rubric should definitely reflect the level the student is performing at and, in an ideal world, whether a student has mastered that skill to the point of enduring understanding. In other words, if the rubric shows that the student understands how to determine the mass of an object, you would hope she would be able to show mastery of this skill in later performances.

To obtain *construct validity*, a rubric must accurately address the skills you are trying to measure, capturing the learning objectives of the lesson. Ideally, if a teacher has four learning objectives, there should be a way to measure each of these in the rubric. A teacher does not always have to use a single rubric, however. You might use multiple rubrics or other assessments throughout the lesson to determine mastery, but by the end of the lesson, all of the objectives should have been evaluated.

In order to have confidence that a rubric is valid (and therefore the inferences we make based on the evaluation are valid), all three kinds of validity evidence should be considered (see Table 1).

In addition to the three C's, there is the *face validity* of a rubric. This is simply making sure that the rubric has the appearance of validity. If you give the rubric to someone and he or she does not believe it looks like it will measure what is intended to measure, he or she is going to have difficulty using it in an objective manner. If you have content, criterion, and construct validity present, you are more likely to have face validity, but not always. If someone else is using your rubric, it needs to be designed so that he or she can look at it and have the belief that it is a valid rubric.

Why You Need Both (Reliability and Validity)

When creating assessments, reliability and validity are essential. Without these components, rubrics are too subjective and will lead to an incorrect measure of a student's mastery. This may seem like common sense, but an assessment audit will reveal many rubrics that are either unreliable or, worse, invalid. The same goes for other assessments used by teachers. Even a multiple-choice test has to have validity and reliability.

Here is an example of a multiple-choice question lacking either validity or reliability:

> What is the point of view in a text?
> a. the setting of the story
> b. the perspective the story is told from
> c. the action the story hinges on
> d. a prediction the story makes

The question is designed to measure the following sixth-grade reading standard for literature from the Common Core State Standards for English Language Arts: "Explain how an author develops the point of view of the narrator or speaker in a

TABLE 1
Three Types of Validity

Type of Validity	Definition	Example
Content	The extent to which the content of the rubric matches the instructional objectives.	If a teacher seeks to measure a student's ability to work in a group, is the teacher considering the many factors that go into making this happen and reflecting these in the language of the rubric? Although you would not be able to capture all of these factors, you would need to break the rubric down enough to show the evaluator a clear picture of what the ability to work in a group looks like.
Criterion	The extent to which scores on the rubric are in agreement with (concurrent validity) or predict (predictive validity) an external criterion.	A student demonstrates that he is at a certain level of mastery when it comes to making an argument. When given a different argument later on, this student demonstrates he is still at this level of mastery.
Construct	The extent to which a rubric corresponds to other variables, as predicted by some rationale or theory.	A lesson has three learning objectives: to learn about integers, to give a presentation, and to work in a group. Yet the rubric is missing one of more of these objectives, meaning all of the objectives are not being measured even though they were a focus of the lesson.

text" (National Governors Association for Best Practices & Council of Chief State School Officers, 2010).

Do you think the question lacks validity and/or reliability?

This question certainly contains terms from the standard, "point of view" and "text." If a student gets this question correct, he would demonstrate that he knows the definition of *point of view*. The question is reliable, but is it valid? This question is invalid according to the definition of *content validity*. The question does not address the standard it aims to assess. The question is supposed to measure whether a student is able to explain how an author develops point of view of the narrator or speaker in a text. The question can be made more valid with a few changes:

Which of the following is a method an author would use to develop point of view in a text?
  a. choosing to use dialogue and revealing the character's thoughts

    b.   choosing a setting that directly affects the story

    c.   choosing an antagonist that is sympathetic to the audience

    d.   choosing a narrator that is interesting to the audience

This question now is both reliable and valid. The student has to look at the different choices and determine a strategy the author needs to use to develop point of view.

The most important aspect of writing any assessment is to make sure it shows consistent results (reliability) and that the skill and level of understanding the standard requires the student to demonstrate is addressed (validity). This can be done in a rubric. You just need to be cognizant as you are writing it, as well as check it over before giving it to students or evaluators.

Assessing This Chapter

To see if you can recognize validity and reliability, complete Reader Assessment 5 (on the following page).

READER ASSESSMENT 5

Example 1: Would you describe this picture as representing *valid*, *reliable*, both, or neither?

Example 2: Would you describe this picture as representing *valid*, *reliable*, both, or neither?

Example 3: Would you describe this picture as representing *valid*, *reliable*, both, or neither?

Answer Key

Example 1 is best characterized as reliable, but invalid. The attempts to hit the target land consistently in the same place. The problem is that they are missing the mark—some even missing the target all together.

Example 2 is valid but unreliable. The attempts to hit the target all reach the target, which means they are all measured correctly. However, the scattered nature of the attempts does not make them very accurate, thus causing the attempts to lack any sort of reliability.

Example 3 features both valid and reliable results. The target is reached by each attempt, making them valid, and the accuracy of the attempts is reliable. There is consistency because all of the attempts make it into the center target and they measure what they are supposed to.

Chapter

5

How to Write a Rubric

This chapter describes, step-by-step, how you can create an objective rubric for use in your classroom. The chapter guides you through developing an analytical, task-specific rubric. The skills used to create the rubric, however, can also be applied to a general, holistic rubric that is single-point.

The Elements of Your Rubric

The best way to create a rubric that is both valid and reliable is by following these three words: Keep it simple (Stanley, 2014). There are some basic parameters to think about when creating your rubric that allow you to keep it simple. Herman, Aschbacher, and Winters (1992) described the following elements:

1. one or more traits or dimensions that serve as the basis for judging students' responses,
2. definitions and examples to clarify the meaning of each trait or dimension, and
3. a scale of values on which to rate each dimension.

In the spirit of keeping it simple, each of these elements can be shortened. When developing a rubric, one must determine the:

1. stated objectives,

2. specific performance characteristics, and
3. range of the performance.

Herman et al. (1992) described a fourth element as well—"Standards of excellence for specified performance levels accompanied by models or examples of each level"—or, in simpler terms, "Exemplars." We will address exemplars later, but the first three elements definitely factor into the construction of your objective rubric. Mapped out on the rubric, they look like Figure 19. Notice that there are only three of each of these elements. You could certainly have more ranges of performance, more stated objectives, and more specific performance characteristics, but sticking with the idea of keeping it simple, three elements are plenty to accomplish what you need to with your rubric.

The Steps to Creating Your Rubric

There are six simple steps to creating a rubric (Stanley, 2014):
✓ **Step 1:** Decide the range of performance.
✓ **Step 2:** Create stated objectives.
✓ **Step 3:** Provide specific performance characteristics in each category.
✓ **Step 4:** Have a tiered system for the performance characteristics.
✓ **Step 5:** Make sure the characteristics are specific and not vague.
✓ **Step 6:** Check for face validity.

Step 1: Decide the Range of Performance

To determine range of performance, as stated before, keep it simple (Stanley, 2014). Give yourself three ranges to consider. Because grades are typically divided up into five ranges (A–F), you may be tempted to do more, but three simplifies the process. Simplifying the rubric provides you with the ability to evaluate and assess quickly. Too many categories will slow you down. Two is too few, in that you are limited to only a couple of performance qualities. You may want to have more options than that. As an example, consider an assignment in which students are tasked with presenting a lesson they developed to the class. If we were to put the teaching of the lesson into a rubric, the range of performance might look like Figure 20.

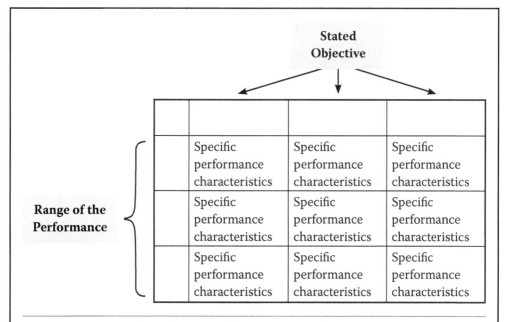

FIGURE 19. Sample rubric template. From *Performance-Based Assessment for 21st-Century Skills* (p. 96), by T. Stanley, 2014, Waco, New York, NY: Routledge Copyright 2014 by Taylor & Francis. Reprinted with permission.

The rubric in Figure 20 has been broken down into "Excellent," "Good," and "Needs Improvement." These categories provide three clear levels of performance. If you want to further define these categories, you can give a range of letter grades, percentages, or point values for each category:
- ✓ Excellent = A
- ✓ Good = B–C
- ✓ Needs Improvement = D–F

Or:
- ✓ Excellent = 90–100
- ✓ Good = 70–89
- ✓ Needs Improvement = 69 and below

How you define levels of performance is up to you and the way you grade in your classroom. Dividing rubrics into ranges of performance allows students to see what a superior project looks like, as well as what to avoid unless they want to end up in the lower categories. Clearly defining that range is very important, however, and this is what the next few steps of rubric creation seek to do.

| Teaching Lesson | | | |
Overall	Organization	Content	Assessment
Excellent			
Good			
Needs Improvement			

Range of the Performance

FIGURE 20. Three ranges of performance. Adapted from *Performance-Based Assessment for 21st-Century Skills* (p. 96), by T. Stanley, 2014, Waco, New York, NY: Routledge Copyright 2014 by Taylor & Francis.. Adapted with permission.

Step 2: Create Stated Objectives

The second step is to create stated objectives. This essentially involves creating categories that identify what you are measuring. The way to think about these is taking the holistic view of the finished product and breaking it down into the parts that, when put together, will equal the whole. If you are trying to evaluate grit, you might think of three things that make up this quality. You could take the definition of grit as supplied by psychologist Angela Duckworth (2016; Duckworth, Peterson, Matthews, & Kelly, 2007), who studied the idea of grit amongst individuals and what characteristics they possessed, and defined grit as perseverance and passion for long-term goals. You could translate this definition into three stated objectives that you could observe in the classroom in order to measure the grit of an individual:

1. risk-taking (passion),
2. overcoming barriers (perseverance), and
3. dependability (long-term goals).

If a student meets one of these stated objectives, she may not possess grit. A student who demonstrates the combination of these objectives, however, may possess grit.

As you create stated objectives, the following tips may be helpful:

✓ Decide how many overall ranges of performance you want to evaluate.

✓ Usually evaluate no less than two (not enough to make objective) ranges of performance and no more than four (gets too confusing).
✓ Try to narrow down the stated objective to a single word or two.
✓ Decide the weight of each category.
✓ You might deem the stated objective that reflects the learning standard to be more important than a minor skill, so you would want to weigh it more in the determination of the final grade.

Going back to our previous example, in which students were tasked with presenting a lesson to the class, the stated objectives for a rubric for this assignment might look like Figure 21. In this rubric, the creator determined that the three stated objectives to focus on were organization, content, and assessment. Note that there are enough categories to break down the overall performance, but not so many that they are impossible to keep track of. Each category can be graded on its own merit, and when you consider all of the objectives, you have the entire picture of how the lesson looked. The objectives are basically like pieces of a puzzle. Separately, the stated objectives show some of the picture, but you have to put them all together in order to see the entire thing.

Step 3: Provide Specific Performance Characteristics

Step 3 is to provide specific performance characteristics for each of the stated objectives. You must clearly define and show what these stated objectives would look like. Again, you are separating the skills into smaller parts to make them easier to see. This is part of how you make the rubric objective. By having all of these measurable descriptions, you can accurately define what mastery is and whether or not the student mastered a task or objective. Some general suggestions for creating your specific performance characteristics include:
✓ Each category should have 2–4 skills that are being evaluated.
✓ As much as possible, these skills should be described with enough detail for the evaluator to be able to envision and understand what they look like.
✓ Start at top range of performance category. By starting with the top range, you can envision the ideal project and set high expectations for students. This creates more rigor and illustrates the level at which you hope students will achieve.

Figure 22 is an example of a specific performance characteristic for the rubric for the assignment in which students were tasked with presenting a lesson to the class. The three descriptions allow the category to be broken down into enough parts so that a student can see which steps need to be accomplished in order to be

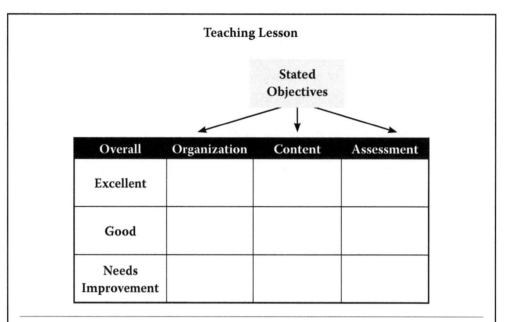

FIGURE 21. Determining stated objectives. Adapted from *Performance-Based Assessment for 21st-Century Skills* (p. 97), by T. Stanley, 2014, Waco, New York, NY: Routledge Copyright 2014 by Taylor & Francis. Adapted with permission.

Teaching Lesson

Overall	Organization	Content	Assessment
Excellent	✓ Lesson is organized in a professional manner; it has a clear beginning, middle, and end, making it easy to follow what is being taught at any given time. ✓ Lesson makes excellent use of time, falling within the 10- to 30-minute range; the student is able to cover all of the important information within the time frame. ✓ Student has all of the necessary materials to teach the lesson and distributes them in an orderly fashion.	Specific Performance Characteristics	
Good			
Needs Improvement			

FIGURE 22. Examples of specific performance characteristics. Adapted from *10 Performance-Based STEM Projects for grades 6–8* (p. 47), by T. Stanley, 2018, Waco, New York, NY: Routledge Copyright 2018 by Taylor & Francis. Adapted with permission.

successful in the category. There is no one thing that will lead the student to success, but rather she will need a combination of several things. For organization, the student knows she will need to focus on three aspects in her lesson in order to be considered excellent. The first characteristic says that the "lesson is organized in a professional manner" and then proceeds to further define what professional manner looks like by adding the detail of "has a clear beginning, middle, and end, making it easy to follow." Without this additional description, one evaluator might have interpreted what a "professional manner" looks like in a different way than someone else. Again, the key to developing these characteristics is being as clear as possible in order to make the rubric objective. For the second characteristic, the rubric gives a clear time frame in which the lesson should be taught, as well as making sure the focus is on the learning objectives. If there had not been parameters to the time of the lesson, you might get a 3-minute lesson or, even worse, an hour-long one. The performance characteristics give both the student presenting the lesson and the evaluator a clear idea of what is expected. The rubric acts as a blueprint for the student. If she constructs her lesson using all three of these stated objectives, she can guarantee herself an excellent rating.

Step 4: Have a Tiered System

Once the bar has been set in the "Excellent" range for a stated objective, it simply becomes a matter of showing what that objective looks like at the other ranges, in this case what "Good" or "Needs Improvement" looks like. The content of the stated objective is the same, but the level with which the student is achieving is where the change occurs. That is when Step 4 comes into play, creating the tier system for the other ranges in the category. A few tips to follow include the following:

✓ Each stated objective should have a matching stated objective at each level. In other words, the skill being assessed should be described on all levels of the range.
✓ Make sure each level is realistic.
✓ The highest range should have high expectations but should not be impossible.
✓ Use the words *but* for "Good" and *not* for "Needs Improvement" in order to scaffold the levels.

Why is having each stated objective at every range of performance level important? Taking the rubric from our example (an assignment in which students were tasked with presenting a lesson to the class), you cannot claim that having the necessary materials for the lesson is important in the "Excellent" range and then omit this requirement from the "Good" and "Needs Improvement" levels. What happens if the student does not have the necessary materials? Similarly, you cannot have something pop up in the "Good" section that was not even considered to be "Excellent." There has to be consistency and fluency in the rubric.

When creating your tiers, the simplest way to think about this is that whenever you go to create a stated objective in the middle category, you add the term *but*, and for the lowest tier you add the term *not*. For example, consider a rubric that assesses students' research skills. At the "Excellent" level, you might include the following stated objective:

> Research is from a reliable source, which is cited, and the student provides specific examples from the research that strengthens his or her position.

This description provides a pretty clear picture of what "Excellent" research looks like, with specific details, such as a reliable source being cited and how the student provides clear examples that strengthen his or her position. If you wanted to take this specific performance characteristic and scaffold it down a tier, you would keep most of the same descriptors, simply tweaking them by inserting the word *but* and describing what less-than-excellent looks like:

> Research seems to be from a reliable source, *but* it is not always cited, and/or the student provides specific examples that don't necessarily strengthen his or her position.

This descriptor is essentially the same statement as that of the "Excellent" range. This descriptor also gives the evaluator some options with the "and/or" statement. For the lower tier, you would take the top tier descriptor and use the word *not* to change its level:

> Research is *not* from a reliable source because it lacks citation, and/or the student does *not* provide specific examples that strengthen his or her position or the examples provided actually weaken his or her position.

A couple of "nots" give the evaluator choices for why the student's work might be at the lower tier.

Figure 23 is what a completed tiered system would look like for our example rubric (for an assignment in which students were tasked with presenting a lesson to the class). The simple difference between the use of details and examples is the use of a *but* or *not*. Here is what this looks like with the third performance characteristic:

Teaching Lesson			
Overall	**Organization**	**Content**	**Assessment**
Excellent	✓ Lesson is organized in a professional manner; it has a clear beginning, middle, and end, making it easy to follow what is being taught at any given time. ✓ Lesson makes excellent use of time, falling within the 10- to 30-minute range; the student is able to cover all of the important information within the time frame. ✓ Student has all of the necessary materials to teach the lesson and distributes them in an orderly fashion.		
Tiered **Good (But)**	✓ Lesson is organized and has a beginning, middle, and end, but it is not always easy to follow. ✓ Lesson makes good use of time, falling within the 10- to 30-minute range, but all of the important learning goals are not covered within the time frame. ✓ Student has all of the necessary materials to teach the lesson, but some time is wasted in how they are distributed.		
Needs Improvement (Not)	✓ Lesson is disorganized; there is no clear beginning, middle, or end. ✓ Lesson does not make good use of time, falling shorter or longer than the 10- to 30-minute range, not covering all of the important details. ✓ Student does not have all of the necessary materials to teach the lesson, wasting time that could be put to better use.		

FIGURE 23. Examples of specific performance characteristics for all tiers. Adapted from *10 Performance-Based STEM Projects for grades 6–8* (pp. 47–48), by T. Stanley, 2018, Waco, New York, NY: Routledge Copyright 2018 by Taylor & Francis. Adapted with permission.

✓ Excellent: Student has all of the necessary materials to teach the lesson and distributes them in an orderly fashion.

✓ Good: Student has all of the necessary materials to teach the lesson, *but* some time is wasted in how they are distributed.

✓ Needs Improvement: Student does *not* have all of the necessary materials to teach the lesson, wasting time that could be put to better use.

Keep in mind these descriptors need to be very clear so that students can follow them. When writing them, you must ask yourself, "What does this characteristic look like?" Sometimes, breaking down the task or lesson into parts like this can be challenging, but if you cannot do it, how can you expect students to be able to do the same?

Step 5: Make Sure the Characteristics Are Specific

Once the first category is complete, repeat the same process for however many stated objectives you decide to evaluate. While you are writing these additional specific performance objectives, keep in mind that the characteristics must be specific. You must avoid vague language. The more specific you are, the more objective your rubric is going to be. The more general you are, the more likely that bias and lack of validity will come into play. Some things to remember include:

✓ You should be able to apply this question to each descriptor: "What does this task/action look like?"
✓ Use specific numbers or a range if the category lends itself to it.
✓ Don't set the bar too high or too low in the wrong range of performance.

Examples of being too vague include using the word *some* in the description of a stated objective, such as "includes some examples." The problem with the word *some* is that it is vague and is subject to much interpretation. Technically, $2 is some money and so is $100, but there is a vast difference between the two. Not to mention the student definition of *some* and the teacher definition might be far apart. A student might define "some examples" as two, while the teacher might think that this means four. Rather than having the student try to guess what the rubric might mean, when applicable, you should use a specific range so that it is clear to the student.

You also need to be careful that the bar is set appropriately in each level and that there is a continuum of performance throughout the entire range. If you set the bar really, really high in the top tier, and then in the middle tier you have described a mediocre performance, the question becomes: How do you assess a good performance that was not quite perfect but would hardly be described as average? A continuum of range of performance might look like Figure 24. See how the numeric descriptors are specific and flow into one another. The presentation is either between the 10- to 15-minute range, a couple of minutes longer or shorter, or several minutes longer or shorter. There is no performance that could not fit into this range.

Step 6: Check for Face Validity

The final step for developing a rubric is to check for face validity. If you have written your specific performance objectives using the steps detailed in this chap-

Speech
✓ The speech uses five effective and meaningful visual aids.
✓ All four group members contribute to the speech.
✓ The speech is within the 10- to 15-minute range.
✓ The speech uses five visual aids, but not all are effective and meaningful.
✓ Three of the group members contribute to the speech but not everyone.
✓ The speech is just a couple of minutes longer or shorter than the 10- to 15-minute range.
✓ The speech does not have at least five visual aids, or all of the visual aids lack meaning and are ineffective.
✓ Only one to two groups members speak; the others do not participate in the speech.
✓ The speech is several minutes longer or shorter than the 10- to 15-minute range.

FIGURE 24. Example continuum of range of performance.

ter, chances are that your rubric is going to be both valid and reliable. However, this does not mean that your rubric is going to pass the eyeball test. The teacher, or whoever is evaluating the performance, has to be able to use this tool effectively. If there is difficulty in using it, the rubric will not be an effective way to capture the performance because it lacks user-friendliness.

There are a few things you can do to determine whether your rubric passes the eyeball test. Some of these include:

  ✓ Look over each stated objective, going through each of the specific performance objectives to be sure they flow and make sense. Especially look to see if you can spot the continuum of performance easily.
  ✓ Practice grading a performance and see how practical the rubric is (maybe during a dress rehearsal, after a first draft is developed, or another venue).
  ✓ Another set of eyeballs is always a good idea. You might be too close to the process to see your final work objectively. You may only see the hard work you have put into it. Have another teacher, or even your students, look it over for any mistakes.

Take your draft of the completed rubric and check it over using these suggestions. Sometimes you will check for face validity and be convinced that your rubric is going to be a success, only to discover problems that only appear when the rubric is actually being used in the field. The rubric may have an unrealistic range, describe a skill that is not really evident in assessment, overlook a skill completely, or have another related issue. In any case, evaluate the performance with what you have and make the changes the next go around. Holding students accountable for something that was not included in the rubric you gave them ahead of time is unfair. Be sure to make notes on your rubric while any possible revisions are fresh in your mind. If you wait until the next school year, some of these issues might have eluded you.

Using all six steps, Figure 25 is the complete rubric for our example assignment (in which students were tasked with presenting a lesson to the class).

Assessing the Chapter

Now that you have reviewed the steps to making your own rubric, you should practice doing so. Make your own rubric. When finished, use Reader Assessment 6 (on p. 67) to evaluate whether you followed all of the steps correctly.

Teaching Lesson

Student: _____   Topic: _____

Overall	Organization	Content	Assessment
Excellent	✓ Lesson is organized in a professional manner; it has a clear beginning, middle, and end, making it easy to follow what is being taught at any given time. ✓ Lesson makes excellent use of time, falling within the 10- to 30-minute range; the student is able to cover all of the important information within the time frame. ✓ Student has all of the necessary materials to teach the lesson and distributes them in an orderly fashion.	✓ Learning goals are clearly laid out and referred to throughout the course of the lesson. ✓ Lesson format is meaningful to the content presented, adding much to understanding of the content. ✓ Lesson covers more than just basics, taking students to a deeper level of understanding.	✓ Assessment evaluates whether the students truly gained mastery of the lesson topic. ✓ Assessment format allows for the "teacher" to truly assess mastery of the learning goals. ✓ Assessment is objective; clear criteria are outlined for how it will be evaluated.
Good	✓ Lesson is organized and has a beginning, middle, and end, but it is not always easy to follow. ✓ Lesson makes good use of time, falling within the 10- to 30-minute range, but all of the important learning goals are not covered within the time frame.	✓ Learning goals are mentioned and referred to occasionally throughout the lesson, but they are not focused on enough. ✓ Lesson format is appropriate to the content presented, providing a basic vehicle for the lesson.	✓ Assessment evaluates whether the students truly gained a basic understanding of the topic but not full mastery. ✓ Assessment format allows the "teacher" to truly assess what students have learned, but whether mastery was attained.

FIGURE 25. Example complete rubric. Adapted from *10 Performance-Based STEM Projects for grades 6–8* (pp. 47–48), by T. Stanley, 2018, Waco, New York, NY: Routledge Copyright 2018 by Taylor & Francis. Adapted with permission.

Overall	Organization	Content	Assessment
Good, *continued*	✓ Student has all of the necessary materials to teach the lesson, but some time is wasted in how they are distributed.	✓ Lesson covers the basics, but does not take students to a deeper level of understanding.	✓ Assessment is mostly objective; clear criteria are outlined for how it will be evaluated, but opinion occasionally counts more than actual skills.
Needs Improvement	✓ Lesson is disorganized; there is no clear beginning, middle, or end. ✓ Lesson does not make good use of time, falling shorter or longer than the 10- to 30-minute range, not covering all of the important details. ✓ Student does not have all of the necessary materials to teach the lesson, wasting time that could be put to better use.	✓ Learning goals are not mentioned, or if they are, they are not referred to during the course of the lesson, causing confusion. ✓ Lesson format is inappropriate for the content, causing a misunderstanding of the topic. ✓ Lesson does not cover the basics, leaving out many important details.	✓ Assessment does not evaluate whether the students gained any understanding of the topic. ✓ Assessment format does not allow the "teacher" to assess what students have learned. ✓ Assessment is subjective; clear criteria are not outlined for how it will be evaluated, or criteria often count opinion more than actual skills.

FIGURE 25. Continued.

READER ASSESSMENT 6

Overall	Set Up	Content	Face Validity
Excellent	✓ Rubric has a distinctive range of performance that clearly shows how the grade will be established. ✓ There are clear, stated objectives that outline the performance and that, when put together, represent the whole. ✓ There are enough specific performance characteristics in each section to give a clear breakdown of the skill.	✓ Rubric has performance characteristics that show what the assignment/performance should look like. ✓ The language used is specific enough to distinguish differences and avoids general terms. ✓ The writing is easy to follow and free from grammatical and spelling errors, making for a professional-looking rubric.	✓ At a glance, you can easily see how the various sections are divided up. ✓ You can clearly see how the specific performance characteristics form a continuum, each one leading into the other. ✓ The rubric is organized; it is clear where and how to evaluate specific skills.
Good	✓ Rubric has a range of performance that gives a good idea of how the grade will be established, but there might be small gaps. ✓ There are clear, stated objectives that outline the performance, but when put together, would not represent the whole. ✓ Most of the stated objectives have enough specific performance characteristics in each section to give a clear breakdown of the skill, but a couple could be broken down further.	✓ Rubric, for the most part, has performance characteristics that show what the assignment/performance would look like, but there are a few unclear characteristics. ✓ The language distinguishes differences and avoids general terms for most of the rubric, but there are a couple of sections that need to be clearly defined.	✓ You have to study the rubric for a moment, but eventually you can see how the various sections are divided up. ✓ You can clearly see how most of the specific performance characteristics form a continuum, each one leading into the other, but a couple jump around too much or do not connect. ✓ You can figure out where and how to evaluate most specific skills, but you have to search for a couple.

Overall	Set Up	Content	Face Validity
Good, *continued*		✓ Most of the writing is easy to follow and free from grammatical and spelling errors, but there are a few clunky sentences or spelling errors that prevent the rubric from looking professional.	
Needs Improvement	✓ Rubric does not have a distinctive range of performance, making it difficult to figure out how the grade will be established. ✓ Objectives define the performance, but when put together, do not paint a clear picture of the whole. ✓ There are more than a few specific performance characteristics that do not break down the skill enough.	✓ The performance characteristics do not give a good idea of what the assignment/performance would look like. ✓ The language used is too general in many areas, leaving a lot of room for subjectivity. ✓ The writing is not always easy to follow and/or has so many grammatical and spelling errors that it is hard to read.	✓ You cannot easily see how the various sections are divided up; the rubric blends them all together. ✓ The specific performance characteristics do not form a continuum, leaving gaps and disjointedness. ✓ It is difficult to determine where and how to evaluate specific skills.

Assessing Rubrics

The Good, the Bad, and the Ugly

With all of your knowledge about rubrics, the most important concept to understand is how to determine whether a rubric is good or not. This applies not only to your own rubrics, but also to other rubrics you might encounter in your teaching experience. This chapter will present eight different rubrics and then ask you to determine their effectiveness—whether they are good, bad, or ugly.

Using the Subjectivity Scale

To help you with your evaluation, use the Subjectivity Scale (see Figure 26). The beautiful thing about rubrics is that they, themselves, are a performance assessment. Because of this, you can use a rubric to determine whether a rubric is as good as it could be. The Subjectivity Scale helps an evaluator look for any subjectivity that would hurt the reliability and validity of a rubric. This will make the rubric as objective as possible. The higher a rubric is on the Subjectivity Scale, the more subjective it is, so you want to make and find rubrics that are in the 2 to 1 range.

The Subjectivity Scale	
5	Rubric provides little to no guidance about what the task/skill being evaluated looks like, leaving the rating open to the evaluator's interpretation. Similarly, there is little guidance on how to score the rubric; the rubric fails to provide a range of performance and instead leaves the evaluator to guess what is appropriate.
4	Rubric contains lots of general terms or fails to define them, so that the evaluator has to make a lot of assumptions about terms. There is also an imbalance in the various categories, meaning minor demonstrations of skills inflate the overall grade and make it look like the student did better on the main learning objective than he or she actually did.
3	Rubric contains a mix of general terms and detailed descriptions that provide the evaluator with lots of guidance on some aspects, but very little on others. The categories are fairly balanced, but it is difficult to discern what is the main learning objective as opposed to ancillary ones. This rubric would allow the evaluator to arrive at a grade, but grading might not be consistent from evaluation to evaluation.
2	Most of the specific performance characteristics are clear in what the task/skill being evaluated looks like. There are a few of these, however, that still leave too much interpretation but not so much that they invalidate the rubric. Rubric also provides fairly balanced categories—the main learning objective is clear, although some minor objectives are weighted too heavily. With a few word and range changes, this rubric would be much more objective and thus better to use with students.
1	Rubric features specific language that paints a clear picture of what each task/skill is supposed to look like. The range of performance is clearly laid out, making it easy for the evaluator to know how to rate a student's work. There is also a balance evident between the various tasks/skills—the more important aspects are weighted more heavily than minor ones. The grade consistently reflects a holistic view of the learning objectives.

FIGURE 26. The subjectivity scale.

Assessing Sample Rubric 1

Sample Rubric 1 (see Figure 27) was designed for assessing a poetry project. This rubric has a lot of terms and numbers, but not much in the way of specificity. Other than the use of an exclamation point, what does the rubric mean by "engaging"? *Engaging* is a very subjective term. A movie one person might find engaging, another person may not. There needs to be more description, so that any evalua-

---

Poetry Project Rubric

Poem Analysis:
Five poetic terms discussed   _____ / 35
Five poetic terms used   _____ / 25
Total   _____ / 60

Presentation:
Music played   _____ / 15
Engaging!   _____ / 5
Total   _____ / 20

Flyer:
Creativity   _____ / 10
Clarity   _____ / 10
Total   _____ / 20

Total Score: _____ / 100

FIGURE 27. Sample rubric 1.

---

tor using this rubric understands what to look for in a student's performance. The same can be said for the use of the term *creativity*. This rubric needs to show what creativity looks like. In regard to the poetry assignment this rubric may be used to assess, creativity might include the imagery, the rhyme scheme, or the subject matter used in the poem. There are also some terms in the rubric that provide no guidance, such as "Music played." What does that even mean? Does that mean the music was physically played? "Music played" is listed out of 15 points, so does that mean students either got a 0 or a 15? There is also some ambiguity about the difference between five poetry terms being discussed and five poetry terms being used. Does "terms discussed" mean that the definition of the poetry term is mentioned, and then "terms used" is the application of that term? This could very well be the case, but the amount of guessing involved increases this rubric's subjectivity.

Where does this rubric fall on the subjectivity scale? This rubric provides little guidance for the evaluator. The bigger problem, however, is how the grade is determined. The rubric makes obvious that the poem analysis is the major focus of this performance because it is worth more points than the presentation and flyer put together. Unclear is the level of quality needed to score certain points. If a student discusses five terms but does so with minimal information, does that meet the requirement of the 35 points, or are there different levels of quality related to discussing the five terms? There is no evidence in this rubric of which of these is the case, again requiring the evaluator to make decisions for him- or herself, which leads to increased subjectivity. Because there is so much guesswork involved in using this rubric, you could have a wide range of final scores. If one evaluator deems that simply hearing five poetry terms gives a student full credit, the evaluator would give this student a score of 35. If another evaluator begins to judge the quality of the terms discussed, a student could include all five terms but only get 2 points for each one, leaving the student with a score of 10. That is a huge discrepancy. That would put this rubric on Level 5 of the Subjectivity Scale.

This rubric is not quite ugly, but it is rather bad. You could put this rubric down in front of someone and he could figure out a way to use it. The biggest problem, of course, is that how an evaluator might use the rubric could end up being very different from its unclear intent. That means that there may be vastly different scores given to similar performances, making the rubric very unreliable.

Assessing Sample Rubric 2

Sample Rubric 2 (see Figure 28) was designed for assessing a research paper assignment related to a career of student interest. As a part of the assignment, students were provided with an outline to follow as they wrote the paper. They also were tasked with conducting an interview with an expert in their field of interest and including the findings from the interview in the paper. This rubric does a decent job of stating specific performance characteristics. The very first one states, "Paper follows the outline clearly," which is clarified further with this description, "allowing the reader to understand what is being discussed at any given time." This additional descriptor paints a clear picture of what successfully following the outline would look like, making for a fairly objective performance characteristic.

Many of the specific performance characteristics show what the various levels of performance would look like, but there are a few that are a little too subjective, such as the one that reads, "Student provides plenty of examples to support statements made in the paper." The subjectivity is in the term *plenty*. Students and evaluators could interpret this differently, resulting in one person thinking the definition of *plenty* is five examples, while another characterizes it as three. Similarly, the first description in the "Paper" category uses the word *few* to describe the amount of grammatical and spelling errors that are permitted to still be "A" work. You do not have to replace these with specific numbers; you just need to have a more defined term. If it were to read instead, "Student provides at least one example for every statement made in the paper, sometimes more," you can see this a little more clearly than the descriptor used before.

Career Paper			
Overall	**Content**	**Paper**	**Research**
A	✓ Paper follows the outline clearly, allowing the reader to understand what is being discussed at any given time. ✓ Student provides plenty of examples to support statements made in the paper. ✓ Student provides much detail, explaining concepts and ideas so that the reader can gain a full understanding of the topic.	✓ Paper has few to no spelling/grammatical errors. ✓ Paper is typed in the correct format. ✓ Paper uses sentence structures that make the paragraphs flow and easy to read.	✓ Research is consistently paraphrased/put into the student's own words. ✓ Expert interview is used throughout the paper, adding insight and depth to the information discussed. ✓ Student uses specific facts and data when necessary, giving the reader a clear understanding of the career.
B–C	✓ Paper follows the outline, but doesn't always allow the reader to understand what is being discussed at any given time. ✓ Student provides examples to support statements in most cases, but not consistently. ✓ Student provides detail, explaining concepts and ideas so that the reader can gain an understanding of the topic, but details could be clearer.	✓ Paper has the occasional spelling/grammatical error; student makes more than a handful of mistakes. ✓ Paper is typed, but not always in the correct format. ✓ Paper mostly uses sentence structures that make the paragraphs easy to read, but some sentences are confusing.	✓ Research is paraphrased/put into the student's own words most of the time. ✓ Expert interview is used sporadically throughout the paper, not providing much insight and depth to the information discussed. ✓ Student uses facts and data, but not always with enough specificity.

FIGURE 28. Sample rubric 2. Adapted from *10 Performance-Based Projects for the Science Classroom* (pp. 81–82), by T. Stanley, 2017, Waco, New York, NY: Routledge Copyright 2017 by Taylor & Francis. Adapted with permission.

Overall	Content	Paper	Research
D–F	✓ Paper does not follow the outline, causing confusion for the reader. ✓ Student provides few to no examples to support statements. ✓ Student does not provide much detail, causing confusion for the reader.	✓ Paper has many spelling/grammatical errors. ✓ Paper is typed sloppily, making it difficult to read. ✓ Paper uses unclear sentence structures, making the topic unclear.	✓ Research is not paraphrased/put into the student's own words most of the time. ✓ Expert interview is barely used in the paper, not providing any insight and depth to the information discussed. ✓ Student does not use facts and data when necessary, leaving the reader with more questions than answers.

FIGURE 28. Continued.

This rubric is a Level 2 on the Subjectivity Scale, making it a good rubric, but maybe not great. Some of the scoring may be invalid or unreliable because the evaluator has to interpret several general statements.

Assessing Sample Rubric 3

Sample Rubric 3 (see Figure 29) might be used to evaluate a student's performance during a presentation to the class about a selected topic. This rubric breaks both the stated objectives and the range of scores into four parts. There is definitely scaffolding from one range to the next. The "Application" category goes from high degree of skill, to considerable skill, to moderate skill, to emerging skill. What is the discernable difference between high degree and considerable . . . or between moderate and emerging? There is a lot of gray here, and there is not enough detail to show the evaluator what these different ranges look like. There would be way too much subjectivity, putting this rubric at a Level 5 on the Subjectivity Scale.

Another problem is the scoring of the rubric. Looking at the way this particular one was scored, the student had two scores that were "Effective," while the other

	Level 4 Exceptional	Level 3 Effective	Level 2 Acceptable	Level 1 Developing
Knowledge/ **Understanding**		X		
Demonstrates an understanding of the topic	Thorough understanding	Considerable understanding	Moderate understanding	Emerging understanding
Communication		X		
Addresses the audience and speaks clearly with structure and purpose	High degree of structure and purpose	Considerable structure and purpose	Moderate structure and purpose	Emerging sense of structure and purpose
Application				X
Exercises skills such as timing, pacing, questioning, and reasoning	High degree of skill	Considerable skill	Moderate skill	Emerging skill
Inquiry/Thinking			X	
Develops and supports an original idea or opinion about a topic	Thorough development and support	Considerable development and support	Moderate development and support	Emerging sense of development and support
Overall Grade: **9/16 = 56%**				

FIGURE 29. Sample rubric 3.

two were "Acceptable" and "Developing." When you look at the terms *effective* and *acceptable*, you do not think about a low grade. You might more commonly consider "Effective" to be in the B range, while "Acceptable" might translate to a C. There is one score in the "Developing" range, making one low marking. Averaging two B's, a C, and a D or F would probably equate to a high C, and yet when you add up the scores provided in this rubric, the student is in the F range with a 56%. The overall grade does not truly match the details of the assignment. Something in this rubric is getting lost in translation. Probably most troubling is the way the evaluator indicated the level of performance, simply putting an X on the general statement that provides absolutely no feedback as to why that level was marked and what could be done to get to the higher level. Grading of rubrics is further covered in Chapter 8. Although this rubric makes it is easy to see and find the various labels, the labels are so general that one would get lost in trying to find where to put an evaluation, making this an ugly rubric.

Assessing Sample Rubric 4

Sample Rubric 4 (see Figure 30) was designed to assess a student-created brochure about a planet as a part of a unit on the solar system. At a glance, Sample Rubric 4 passes the face validity test. The rubric's different descriptions provide enough detail to show what each level looks like. The performance objectives have been correlated to a number, meaning that when the evaluator determines how the performance aligns with each objective, that will provide a numerical score that can then be added up to provide a total. These detailed descriptions would earn no more than a Level 2 on the Subjectivity Scale, which is pretty good. The problem with this rubric, however, comes in the balance of the scoring.

The way this rubric is set up, a student could max out on certain categories because he or she is creative and makes an attractive brochure that is written with proper grammar and spelling. This would give the student 16 points. The academic content, however, could be totally missing or completely incorrect, and yet this student would still receive no worse than a B on the brochure. The final gradebook would show that this student has a mastery of the science content—when, in fact, he does not. That means this rubric is unreliable. That would place this rubric at a Level 4 on the Subjectivity Scale because of the "imbalance in the various categories."

That would make this a bad rubric. The good news is that with just an addition to the scoring, this rubric could become a lot more reliable. If the rubric scored the four ancillary skills of creativity, attractiveness, and writing on the current scale of 1, 2, 3, or 4, but upped the point total for the academic content to 5, 10, 15, or 20, then the science content the student displays would account for more than half of the grade, making it impossible to get anything above a 40% without knowledge of the science content.

Alternatively, if this was a brochure for an art class whose teacher is trying some crosscurricular material, that would certainly up the reliability because the skills the teacher wanted to focus on were the creativity and attractiveness, not the science content.

Solar System PBL Planet Brochure Rubric

Category	4	3	2	1
Academic Content: Realism	Five or more facts have been accurately used. Information was clearly explained and easy to understand.	Four facts have been used. Information was clearly explained and easy to understand.	Two to three facts have been used. Information was somewhat clear and might have been difficult to understand.	Fewer than two facts have been used. Information was unclear and difficult to understand.
Creativity: Fantasy	Five or more fictional pieces of information have been used and relate directly to the facts presented.	Four fictional pieces of information have been used and relate to the facts presented.	Two to three fictional pieces of information have been used and might relate to the facts presented.	Fewer than two fictional pieces of information have been used that do not relate to the facts presented.
Creativity: Graphics and Pictures	Seven or more graphics have been included. Graphics relate to the text and represent a variety of images.	Five to six graphics have been included. Graphics relate to the text and represent a variety of images.	Three to four graphics have been included. Some graphics relate to the text.	Fewer than three graphics have been included. Graphics do not completely relate to the text.
Attractiveness and Organization	The brochure is very persuasive and has attractive formatting, and the information is well organized.	The brochure is persuasive and has attractive formatting, and the information is well organized.	The brochure is somewhat persuasive. Organization of the information might be confusing to the reader.	The brochure is not persuasive. Organization of information is confusing to the reader.
Writing: Grammar	There are very few grammar, capitalization, punctuation, or spelling errors.	The are some grammar, capitalization, punctuation or spelling errors that do not affect the meaning.	There are some grammar, capitalization, or spelling errors that might affect the meaning.	There are many grammar, capitalization, punctuation, or spelling errors that affect the meaning.

Overall Brochure Score: _____ /20

_____ %

FIGURE 30. Sample rubric 4.

Assessing Sample Rubric 5

As you can see in Sample Rubric 5 (see Figure 31), there is a lot going on, and that is its major issue: It is too busy. This rubric fails miserably on the face validity test. It is just plain ugly. Someone trying to use this in the classroom while students are giving their performance would have much difficulty. There are 12 specific characteristics under the "Artistic Product" section. How on Earth would someone be able to catch all 12 of these, much less properly evaluate them? Because of the major issues with the face validity, this bleeds into the actual validity of the rubric. Undoubtedly, while trying to evaluate a student, some things would be overlooked. That means skills that were meant to be measured would be missed, or, because the rater would have to work so fast, certain skills would not be evaluated properly.

In addition, the language is too vague in many places. Some examples of this are:

✓ Presentation flowed/Presentation somewhat flowed/Presentation was fragmented
✓ Presentation was organized throughout/Presentation was mostly organized throughout/Presentation was disorganized throughout
✓ Presentation was engaging/Presentation was generally engaging/Presentation was not engaging

There are even times when the different ranges of performance do not change from tier to tier. Overall, this rubric is rated a Level 3 on the Subjectivity Scale because there are some specific performance characteristics that are detailed and clearly show what they would look like, but too many are general.

Assessing Sample Rubric 6

Sample Rubric 6 (see Figure 32) is a one-point rubric for evaluating a model of an escape room intended to help students review for their math test. It is a nicely laid out rubric, as the stated objectives correspond with their specific performance characteristics. The specific performance characteristics also are well described. Under the "Clues/Creativity" section is the following description:

✓ Each clue was thoughtfully hidden and had a purpose within the room.
✓ The clues were the right level of difficulty (required thought and creativity to create and solve).
✓ Clues were connected to the math problems through a creative avenue.

Market Day Presentation Rubric

	Content Points ____ x 2 = ____	Artistic Product Points ____ x 2 = ____	Presentation x 1 = ____
Great (9–10)	**Trailer:** ✓ Provides detailed plot preview through acting ✓ Narration and/or dialogue appropriately details main story and themes ✓ Conflict(s) is deliberately stated and/or acted in trailer ✓ Questions and soliloquies provide insight to conflict(s) ✓ Ending provides conclusion to the play's conflict **Movie Poster:** ✓ Visually depicts complex theme(s) of play ✓ Presenters clearly explain complex theme(s) **Visual Depiction:** ✓ Depiction symbolically represents overall theme(s) ✓ Presenters clearly explain the symbols and their significance to the play	✓ All aspects of presentation are visually pleasing ✓ Speakers are easily heard by all ✓ Artistic products are easily seen ✓ Artistic products are an excellent representation of the play's overall theme(s) ✓ Each product is neatly done ✓ Each product is done with creative elements ✓ Characters and presenters stayed in character and were focused ✓ Section were integrated with each other ✓ Presentation flowed ✓ Presentation was engaging ✓ Participants showed enthusiasm/passion about the play ✓ Overall story was clearly told by all participants	✓ Presentation was organized throughout ✓ Participants spoke clearly and enthusiastically ✓ Each participant's effort is clearly noted in performance ✓ Each section was performed within the appropriate time frame ✓ Transitions between the different facets of the presentation were smooth

FIGURE 31. Sample rubric 5.

	Content Points ___ x 2 = ___	Artistic Product Points ___ x 2 = ___	Presentation x 1 = ___
Good (7–8)	**Trailer:** ✓ Provides detailed plot preview through acting ✓ Narratives and dialogue detail main story and themes ✓ Conflict(s) is stated and/or acted in trailer ✓ Famous quotations and/or soliloquies were included ✓ Ending provides conclusion to the play's conflict **Movie Poster:** ✓ Visually depicts complex theme(s) of play ✓ Presenters clearly explain complex theme(s) **Visual Depiction:** ✓ Depiction represents overall theme(s) of the play ✓ Presenters explain theme(s) and their significance to the play	✓ Most aspects of presentation are visually pleasing ✓ Most speakers are easily heard by all ✓ Artistic products can be seen ✓ Artistic products represent the play's overall theme(s) ✓ Each product is neatly done ✓ Each product is done with creative elements ✓ Characters and presenters stayed in character and were focused most of the time ✓ Some sections were integrated with each other ✓ Presentation somewhat flowed ✓ Presentation was generally engaging ✓ Most participants showed enthusiasm/passion about the play ✓ Overall story was told by all participants	✓ Presentation was mostly organized throughout ✓ Most participants spoke clearly and enthusiastically ✓ Most participants' efforts are clearly noted in performance ✓ Some sections ran a little long/short ✓ Some transitions between the different facets of the presentation were smooth

FIGURE 31. Continued.

	Content Points ___ x 2 = ___	Artistic Product Points ___ x 2 = ___	Presentation x 1 = ___
Needs Work (0–6)	**Trailer:** ✓ Provides little plot preview through acting ✓ Narratives and dialogue rarely detail main story and themes ✓ Conflict(s) is not stated and/or acted in trailer ✓ Quotations and/or soliloquies were not included ✓ Ending does not provide conclusion **Movie Poster:** ✓ Overall theme(s) is not clear ✓ Presenters do not clearly explain the theme(s) **Visual Depiction:** ✓ Depiction does not represent overall theme(s) of the play ✓ Presenters do not explain theme(s) and their significance to the play	✓ Few aspects of presentation are visually pleasing ✓ Most speakers are not easily heard by all ✓ Artistic products cannot be seen ✓ Artistic products do not represent the play's overall theme(s) ✓ Few products are neatly done ✓ Few products are done with creative elements ✓ Characters and presenters did not stay in character and/or were not focused most of the time ✓ Few sections were integrated with each other ✓ Presentation was fragmented ✓ Presentation was not engaging ✓ Few participants showed enthusiasm/passion about the play ✓ Overall story was not told by all participants	✓ Presentation was disorganized throughout ✓ Participants did not speak clearly and enthusiastically ✓ Few participants' efforts are clearly noted in performance ✓ Some sections ran overly long/short or were not included ✓ Transitions were not evident

FIGURE 31. Continued.

Escape Room Rubric

Escape Room Title: _____   Creator's Name: _____

	Below Standard ✓	At Standard	Above Standard ✓
Write the Room		✓ The storyline is engaging and sets the stage for an exciting gaming experience; it allows the reader to understand the concept for the room while providing just enough information to get started ✓ Grade-appropriate grammar and mechanics are applied	
Questions		✓ All 13 questions, one from each lesson, are included ✓ The work on the answer key is accurate and shows all steps	
Clues/ Creativity		✓ Each clue was thoughtfully hidden and had a purpose within the room ✓ The clues were the right level of difficulty (required thought and creativity to create and solve) ✓ Clues were connected to the math problems through a creative avenue	
Organization		✓ Participants are able to successfully find the clues and questions ✓ The life-size clues are neatly organized and easily associated with the hidden clues ✓ The room has a cohesive feel, and everything blends together nicely ✓ Obvious thought to the organization of the clues and room is apparent	
Final Rating and Comments			

FIGURE 32. Sample rubric 6.

These descriptions fall under the range of performance "At Standard," according to the rubric. There is a column for "Above Standard," so that if a student goes above and beyond what is expected, there is flexibility to the rubric. The problem with this particular rubric is that there is really no place to go to be above the standard. If you were developing a one-point rubric, you would want to have basic mastery in the middle, which gives students a chance to shine above what the average student would do. But if you look at the specific performance characteristics just shared, how can you do better than "Each clue was thoughtfully hidden and had a purpose within the room." Could the student be more thoughtful or their clues have more purpose? That would not necessarily make it better, and now you are starting to get into subjective territory, gauging the various levels of thoughtfulness and purpose.

Overall, this rubric would score a Level 2 on the Subjectivity Scale because of its specific descriptions, but unfortunately, the way it is currently written, this is a bad rubric because it loses validity in the accurate measurement of mastery. Its bar is set too high. The writer of this rubric could fix this by setting mastery standards that demonstrate the basic intent of the lesson. These could be rewritten to look like this:

    ✓ Each clue was hidden and was in the room.

    ✓ The clues were neither too easy nor too challenging.

    ✓ Clues were connected to the math problems.

These descriptions fall more in line for what "at standard" means, and allow the evaluator some space to grade above this mastery level if the student displays a stronger performance.

Assessing Sample Rubric 7

Sample Rubric 7 (see Figure 33) has a good balance and flow to it, passing the face validity test. The range of performance is clearly laid out numerically. There is even a little flexibility in that if the rater circles two categories in the 5 range and one in the 3, a 4 could be given to split the difference. The stated objectives are weighted so that students are aware of what the focal point of the learning should be—in this case, math content. There is a lot of "show" rather than "tell" in the specific performance characteristics, which adds to the objectivity. An example is under "Outline":

    ✓ Paper follows the outline clearly (which is the tell), allowing the reader to know what is being discussed at any given time (which is the show).

Math in Real Life Rubric

Students: _____　　　　Topic: _____

Overall	Outline x 2	Math Content x 3	Mechanics x 1
5	✓ Paper follows the outline clearly, allowing the reader to know what is discussed at any given time. ✓ Student provides plenty of examples to support statements made in the paper. ✓ Student provides much detail, explaining concepts and ideas so that the reader can gain a full understanding of what is discussed.	✓ Research is consistently paraphrased/put into student's own words. ✓ Math concept is explained with much detail, showing a complete understanding. ✓ A legitimate job that uses this math is discussed in detail, and there is a clear link to this job and its use of the math concept.	✓ Paper has few to no spelling/grammatical errors. ✓ Paper is typed in the correct format, using double-spaced, 12-point Times New Roman. ✓ Paper uses sentence structures that make the paragraphs flow and easy to read.
3	✓ Paper follows the outline, but doesn't always allow the reader to understand what is discussed at any given time. ✓ Student gives examples to support statements made in the paper, but inconsistently. ✓ Student provides detail, explaining concepts and ideas so that the reader can gain an understanding of what is discussed.	✓ Research is paraphrased/put into student's own words, but student occasionally uses terms and phrases that are not his or her own. ✓ Math concept is explained, showing a basic understanding of it, but a lack of details and/or examples show a lack of depth of understanding.	✓ Paper has the occasional spelling/grammatical errors; includes more than a handful of mistakes. ✓ Paper is typed but not always in the correct format; there are inconsistencies in font, size, style, or spacing. ✓ Paper mostly uses sentence structures that make the paragraphs flow and easy to read, but occasional awkward sentences cause confusion.

FIGURE 33. Sample rubric 7. Adapted from *10 Performance-Based Projects for the Math Classroom* (pp. 126–127), by T. Stanley, 2017, Waco, New York, NY: Routledge Copyright 2017 by Taylor & Francis. Adapted with permission.

Overall	Outline x 2	Math Content x 3	Mechanics x 1
3, *continued*		✓ A legitimate job that uses this math is discussed, and there is a link to this job and its use of the math concept, but the link is not explained clearly enough.	
1	✓ Paper does not follow the outline, causing confusion for the reader. ✓ Student provides few to no examples to support statements made in the paper. ✓ Student does not provide much detail, leaving the reader confused.	✓ Research is, many times, not put into student's own words ✓ Math concept is not explained well, leaving the reader to wonder if the student understands the concept. ✓ Either the job researched does not really use this math much, or there is no link between the job and the math concept.	✓ Paper has many spelling/grammatical errors, making the paper difficult to read. ✓ Paper has inconsistent spacing, style, and size of font, making it difficult to read. ✓ Paper has sloppy sentence structures that make paragraphs unclear and difficult to follow.

Overall Rubric Score: _____ /30

FIGURE 33. Continued.

This is followed throughout the range of performance, employing the "but/not" model:

✓ Paper follows the outline, but doesn't always allow the reader to understand what is being discussed at any given time.

✓ Paper does not follow the outline, causing confusion for the reader.

This pattern of clarifying the statement with a description follows throughout the rubric, making this rubric a Level 1 on the Subjectivity Scale, which makes it valid. Although the "math content" section is specific to this particular project, the "outline" and "mechanics" are universal enough that they could be used on future projects, making this a reliable rubric.

Assessing Sample Rubric 8

Sample Rubric 8 (see Figure 34) is used to evaluate the coloring abilities of a student. It is fairly simply laid out, showing the rater where the range of performance is and the stated objectives. The specific performance characteristics are fairly detailed for the most part. For the stated objective of "Color," each of the descriptions has a clarifying comment:

✓ Colored completely (no white spaces)

✓ Colored almost completely (some white spaces)

✓ Not colored completely (lots of white spaces)

✓ Not colored completely (mostly white spaces)

Right now, this rubric is a Level 1 or 2 on the Subjectivity Scale. If we take out those clarifying comments, watch what happens to their subjectivity:

✓ Colored completely

✓ Colored almost completely

✓ Not colored completely

✓ Not colored completely

Without the clarifying comments, the subjectivity would probably be in the 3–4 range because there is some ambiguity to the performance characteristics. The clarifying comments show you what the description looks like. Knowing specifically what to look for increases objectivity.

The only part that is a bit subjective is the middle stated objective of "Fine Motor Skills." The scale for "marks outside of the lines" is no/few/some/lots. Although specific numbers are not necessary to make this clearer, a more defined word might increase the objectivity: no/few/several/most. This just paints a clearer picture. Overall, this is still a pretty good rubric and one that could be used in the classroom to objectively determine mastery of coloring.

	Well Done 4	Satisfactory 3	Needs Improvement 2	Not Acceptable 1	Score
Color	Colored completely (no white spaces)	Colored almost completely (some white spaces)	Not colored completely (lots of white spaces)	Not colored completely (mostly white spaces)	
Fine Motor Skills	No marks outside of the lines	A few marks outside of the lines	Some marks outside of the lines	Lots of marks outside of the lines	
Use of Color	Uses the correct color for each item	Uses the correct color on eight of the nine items	Uses the correct color on six or seven of the nine items	Uses the correct color on fewer than six items	
				Total:	

FIGURE 34. Sample rubric 8.

Assessing the Chapter

You have done enough assessing in this chapter. Move on to the next. If you ever need an anchoring session on evaluating rubrics, however, revisit this chapter to refresh your thought process. Here are some additional things to think about when reviewing a rubric (adapted from Huba & Freed, 2000):

- ✓ Does the rubric help me to distinguish among the levels of quality in students' work?
- ✓ Are there too many or too few levels of achievement specified?
- ✓ Are the descriptions of performance incomplete or unclear?
- ✓ Are there important aspects of the task missing from the rubric?
- ✓ Do the criteria reflect the content or mastery of the knowledge associated with the student work?
- ✓ Is the process of achieving the learning outcome reflected in the rubric?
- ✓ Will the rubric help students be successful in the learning and assessment processes?
- ✓ Will the rubric help students understand the assessment and evaluation process?
- ✓ Will the rubric provide useful guidance and feedback to students?

Chapter
7

Empowering Students to Write Their Own Rubrics

As you become more confident in your own ability to write effective and objective rubrics, one thing to consider is teaching students how to write them as well. There are a few advantages to this:

- ✓ clarity,
- ✓ ownership,
- ✓ motivation,
- ✓ feedback,
- ✓ efficiency, and
- ✓ instruction.

Advantages of Students Creating Their Own Rubrics

Here is a scene that has happened from time to time in a classroom that uses rubrics. You take the time to thoughtfully create a rubric that is specific to your students' needs. You have tried very hard to make sure it is objective, and you are proud because you know that this rubric will allow you to better determine the learning progress of your students. You go over the lesson with the students, explaining to them what they are going to be doing in order to demonstrate learning. You beam as you hand out your completed rubric that clearly lays out what students need to do in order to be successful. A student takes a quick glance at it, and then stuffs it into his binder to be lost amongst the sea of other papers he has accumulated throughout the school year.

You should not take this personally. Students have become conditioned to receiving reams of paper from their teachers—another sheet of paper just becomes white noise. There is no buy in and no ownership. But you know better. You know that this rubric is important because it is the key to their success. If students would only pay attention to it, the rubric would show them how to get that coveted A. If you could only find some way to get them to look at it, it would prevent misunderstandings and misinterpretations.

Clarity

One way to increase students' chances of looking at and engaging with a rubric is to have them feel like they had a part in its creation. This means that students will care about the rubric more. The rubric is not just something the teacher randomly handed to them. It is something that they put some effort into and had some say in the creation of. Because students are more likely to look at a rubric that they helped to create, they will gain more clarity as to what they are supposed to be doing during the course of a lesson or project. Being involved in the creation of a rubric will enable students to better be able to show mastery and learn a lesson's objectives.

Ownership

The ownership developed by the students becoming stakeholders in the assessment process causes something to happen that can sometimes be difficult to achieve in the classroom: Students will begin to care about what they are doing. This is part of the power of authentic learning, such as problem-based learning, project-based learning, and other forms of inquiry-based learning. These strategies for learning make students part of the process. You make students a part of the process by giving them choice—not only choice in topic or choice in product, but also in how the end result will be assessed. Giving students choice in the assessment by allowing them to help create the rubric is just another entry point for them to feel like they are in control of their own learning and it is not just been dictated to them.

Motivation

Student ownership also helps with motivation. Increased motivation will likely result in better quality work by students. This is because the work becomes not merely another hoop for students to jump through, but they truly see it as something exciting to work on. Students are bound to be more motivated when they have a say in how they are going to be evaluated. It gives them a voice in the process. Because they are motivated, the assignment or performance assessment will be something that they want to do well. In addition to helping students, this motivation helps the teacher because the products that students will turn in will be so much better. Products will be easier to grade because you are more likely to be looking for performance criteria that students met, rather than discern criteria that they did not meet.

The second way motivation helps is the amount of enduring understanding that takes place. Because there is greater student involvement, students will better remember what they learn. There is nothing more frustrating as a teacher than students who memorize the content long enough to take the assessment, but the moment they turn in their test, they have begun to forget their learning. When students help create rubrics they have a better chance of actually learning content rather than just memorizing.

Feedback

Students will get better feedback from a rubric than they will from most traditional assignments, especially if they helped to create it. When students take a multiple-choice test, there just is not much opportunity for feedback. Students either got the questions right or wrong. Rubrics can offer more concrete and useful feedback in a couple of ways. If a specific performance characteristic is written in such a way that it shows what level a student's performance was at, this will provide a lot of feedback. Not only that, the student can look at the performance characteristic above the level that she achieved, if applicable, and see what she could have done to improve her work. Secondly, there is ample opportunity for teachers to put written feedback on a rubric. This will be discussed in much more detail in the next chapter, but rather than just circling or checking a box on the rubric, the evaluator can also write comments about what students did well or what they can work to improve. There is opportunity for verbal feedback as well. When the teacher returns rubrics to students, he can sit down and conference with students individually and offer his observations and opinions. The student can take part in this conversation and also reflect upon any takeaways. Because students helped to develop the rubric, they will have a strong understanding of what the expectations were, why their performances were rated as they were, and how best to utilize any feedback.

Efficiency

One advantage of having students create their own rubrics is efficiency and ease. There are three ways that having students helping create rubrics makes things easier. The most obvious one is division of labor. Now instead of just the teacher working on the rubric, there are others involved in the process. You have multiple opinions and multiple ideas, resulting in things getting done faster. Also, because you are developing the rubric during class time together, you do not have to give up any of your planning or personal time.

The second advantage is that the rubric will likely be of better quality. Students bring all sorts of experiences from their years in school. They can offer many good examples and poor ones that they have seen. This will paint a much clearer picture when it comes to the specific performance characteristics to be outlined in the rubric. Students can help you to shape this vision, and, thus, it will be more obvious what exactly a mastery level performance looks like because everyone is on the same page. In addition, the teacher will have multiple sets of eyes to catch any mistakes. Sometimes when we are making a rubric by ourselves, we fail to see mistakes because we are too close to our work. Another set of eyes might point out if things were overlooked or the possible pitfalls that might occur once the rubric is in use. We sometimes forget that, no matter the age of our students, they often have really good ideas. They might suggest something the teacher did not even think of, bringing another dimension to the rubric.

Third, because the students know what kind of product they will create to display mastery, especially if they are provided with choice, they will be able to help make a rubric that is tailored to their final performance. This is one way that a rubric can better match the intent of a lesson.

Instruction

The final advantage of creating rubrics with your students can be summed up by Dr. Anne Davies: "Setting criteria with students does not take up valuable instruction time—it is instruction" (as cited in Abunassar, Kirkham, & Warkentin, 2015, p. 2).

Learning how to evaluate themselves goes a long way in teaching students how to reflect. This is the space in which some of the most powerful learning comes into play because students will not always have school, their parents, or their mentors to help them to learn. Eventually, our students have to figure out things for themselves and learn from their mistakes. Having the ability to reflect helps students to learn a lesson a lot more effectively.

Creating Rubrics With Students

When creating a rubric collectively as a class, follow the same six steps you would use to create your own rubric. You will create the range of performance, stated objectives, and specific performance characteristics together. The one thing that might have to be added to the process is having students number the specific performance characteristics at each range of performance. This helps them to see how the tier system works and ensures the entire range is covered.

A rubric created with students might look like Figure 35. Notice under "Organization" that the paper "follows a clear, logical order" at the "Excellent level," and the "Good" and "Needs Improvement" ranges also address this criterion described under the number 1. After developing rubrics with students for a while, you can get rid of the numbers if you want, but they are helpful to guide students' thinking in the beginning.

Having students help develop the rubric allows them to see the components that make for a successful performance. This especially helps those students who have trouble seeing the big picture. The dialogue of the class debate on what is a valid description and what is not will also be very enlightening because students develop a clear understanding of acceptable work. As students voice more and more ideas, classmates see concrete examples of what to do and what not to do. For example, a student may say that he dislikes when presenters read the words right off of a PowerPoint slide. Many others in the class agree, and pretty soon the class has created a descriptor that reads "Student presents rather than reads the content of his or her PowerPoint." Because a class discussion was involved, the entire class is aware of this rubric requirement, and the likelihood of a student doing this in their presentation is greatly lessened.

Although the teacher might lead the discussion, being quiet and letting the students arrive at conclusions for themselves can be very powerful. Plus, there is the empowerment of determining for themselves how they are going to be assessed. Most times students have no say in this matter, but, here, you are allowing them input. In most cases, they will arrive at the same decisions you would have made yourself, but in this scenario, they feel as though they had a voice. This allows them to connect to the evaluation process and have a better understanding of how their performance is evaluated. The skill of making a really good, objective rubric is something that can be taught to learners of all ages.

Animal Research Paper

Students: _____   Topic: _____

	Content	Organization	The Why	Grammar
Excellent	1. Student uses lots of good information to complete Sections 2 and 3. 2. Observations for Section 4 are insightful and include student reflection. 3. Student shows a thorough understanding of the topic.	1. Paper follows a clear, logical order. 2. Paper follows the outline completely.	1. Paper answers the "why," giving a complete explanation. 2. Student uses examples to illustrate points and includes lots of detail.	1. Paper has few or no errors in spelling, grammar, or usage. 2. Sentences are organized and make sense, one leading into the next.
Good	1. Student uses some information to complete Sections 2 and 3, but more information could make the paper clearer. 2. Observations for Section 4 are a play-by-play that do not include any student reflections. 3. Student shows an understanding of major points, but a limited understanding of details.	1. Paper follows a clear, logical order, but gets off track sometimes. 2. Paper follows the outline, but some topics are not addressed.	1. Paper answers the "why" in a basic manner, but does not provide a complete explanation. 2. Student uses examples to illustrate points but does not always include enough detail.	1. Paper has many errors in spelling, grammar, or usage. 2. Sentences are organized but do not flow into one another.
Needs Improvement	1. Student does not use much information to complete Sections 2 and 3. 2. Observations for Section 4 are minimal without much described. 3. Student shows a lack of understanding about key points.	1. Paper lacks direction or is confusing. 2. Paper does not follow the outline; many areas are not addressed.	1. Paper does not answer the "why." 2. Student does not use many examples to illustrate points.	1. Paper has many errors in spelling, grammar, or usage that interfere with the meaning of the paper. 2. Sentences are disorganized, and there is no logical flow to the paper.

FIGURE 35. Sample student-created rubric.

Having Students Write Their Own Rubrics

Once you have worked with your students on creating rubrics as a class, you might be ready to have them create their own, personalized rubrics. This opens up another level of learning in the classroom. Instead of all students working on the same product for a lesson, each student can find a product that is meaningful to him or her but will still show mastery of learning. Having students write their own rubrics allows you to offer options in your classroom, which leads to student engagement and creativity.

Benefits of students writing their own rubrics also include the following:
- ✓ The rubric can be tailored to a student's specific performance.
- ✓ Students have complete ownership because they created most of the rubric on their own.
- ✓ You, the teacher, get to have individual conversations with students about what good work looks like.
- ✓ Students come to a greater understanding about specific components of the lesson objectives.
- ✓ Students become more familiar with the rubric language because they have to write it themselves; this makes for a deeper understanding of the expectations and thus better products.

As the teacher, you might provide the range of performance but have students create the stated objectives and specific performance characteristics. You might provide them with a blank rubric, such as Figure 36. You would then give students class time to begin to construct the rubric, deciding the stated objectives and determining what they look like and how they can best be described. Suggest that students do this with pencil, as the rubric will act as a working document that will be edited and changed throughout this process. Depending on their experience or age, you might have to walk students through this the first couple of times before they begin to get the hang of it.

After giving students time to create a rough draft, either collect the student rubrics and look them over, or better yet, sit down with students individually and have a conversation about their rubrics. When looking over the student rubrics, assess them as you would your own, including going through each range of performance, looking through the tiers to be sure the rubric flows and makes sense. If students have been using the numbering system, this will be easier to determine. Some other things to check for include the following:
- ✓ Make sure the rubric is legible.
- ✓ Make sure the rubric shows rather than tells.
- ✓ Check for sloppiness.

Product Rubric			
Overall			
Excellent (A)			
Good (B–C)			
Needs Improvement (D–F)			

FIGURE 36. Example blank rubric template.

- ✓ Look for space to make teacher comments.
- ✓ Help students to use the common language that the class is using for rubrics.
- ✓ Check for reasonable spelling and grammar.

You can choose to use one of the rubrics provided in this book, such as the Subjectivity Scale (see Figure 26, p. 70), for guidance in looking over students' rubrics. First and foremost, much like your own work, you should make sure that the rubrics are valid and reliable. Either through written or verbal feedback, students should be presented with strategies for revising their rubrics to make sure they are usable. These might be minor fixes or major overhauls. Either way, you should provide some guidance as to what the revisions should look like. Then, give students time to revise their rubrics. Have another check-in once they feel that they have revised their rubrics as asked. At this point, either sign off on their rubrics as being acceptable or suggest further revisions. It is important for each student to keep revising until you feel that his or her rubric will properly determine mastery of the lesson.

Sometimes when you ask students to create their own rubrics, there are certain things that you want to make sure all students are going to be evaluated on. You have the option to provide a teacher-created category (see Figure 37). This way students know this is a very important aspect to your class or this assignment.

				Responsibility/Class Time
Excellent				1. Was on task a majority of class time. 2. Made great use of exploration time, using the given time to find many learning opportunities. Came to class fully prepared to work on product with a plan in mind. 3. Turned in second evaluation with detailed comments.
Good				1. Was on track most times, but occasionally got off task. 2. Came to class with what was needed for the product but not always with a plan. 3. Turned in second evaluation but not detailed comments.
Needs Improvement				1. Was off-task several times in class. 2. Made poor use of exploration time; mostly fumbled around finding nothing. 3. Came to class lacking what was needed for the product or didn't plan what to do. 4. Did not turn in second evaluation.

Thermal Energy Project Rubric

Students: _____ Product: _____

FIGURE 37. Sample rubric template with teacher-created category.

Additional Thoughts About Student-Created Rubrics

According to Andrade (1996), in order to have students create rubrics effectively in the classroom, you must meet the following criteria:
1. Have students look at models of good versus "not-so-good" work. A teacher could provide sample assignments of variable quality for students to review.

2. List the criteria to be used in the scoring rubric and allow for discussion of what counts as quality work. Asking for student feedback during the creation of the list also allows the teacher to assess the students' overall writing experiences.

3. Articulate gradations of quality. These hierarchical categories should concisely describe the levels of quality (ranging from bad to good) or development (ranging from beginning to mastery). They can be based on the discussion of the good versus not-so-good work samples or immature versus developed samples. Using a conservative number of gradations keeps the scoring rubric user-friendly while allowing for fluctuations that exist within the average range.

4. Practice on models. Students can test the scoring rubrics on sample assignments provided by the instructor. This practice can build students' confidence by teaching them how the instructor would use the scoring rubric on their papers. It can also aid student/teacher agreement on the reliability of the scoring rubric.

5. Ask for self- and peer-assessment.

6. Revise the work on the basis of that feedback. As students are working on their assignment, they can be stopped occasionally to do a self-assessment and then give and receive evaluations from their peers. Revisions should be based on the feedback they receive.

7. Use teacher assessment, which means using the same scoring rubric the students used to assess their work. (pp. 15–16)

Based on the criteria laid out in this list, it would be safe to assume that if you were to follow the steps laid out for you in Chapter 5, you can teach your students to create rubrics that evaluate skills in your classroom in an objective manner.

Assessing the Chapter

Use Reader Assessment 7 (on the following page) to assess if your class is ready to handle creating rubrics.

READER ASSESSMENT 7

	Do Not Have a Clue	Starting to Get It But Not Quite There	Basic Understanding	Have a Really Good Idea
My students understand how rubrics work and how they help to evaluate their performance.				
My students do a pretty good job helping me to create rubrics as a class.				
My students have a good grasp of the common language used in the class rubrics.				
My students know the difference between showing and telling.				
My students know what tiers of performance look like.				
My students can work independently.				

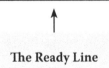

The Ready Line

If a majority of the checkmarks are on the left side of the ready line, students are most likely not ready to create their own rubrics. You might need to revisit some of the concepts or work together to create rubrics as a group so that they become more familiar with these concepts. On the other hand, if most of the markings are to the right of the line, your class is probably ready to go.

Chapter
8

How to Grade Using Your Rubrics

Once a rubric is made, you actually have to use it in the classroom to evaluate students. This involves being able to translate what is recorded on the rubric into a grade or some sort of measurable goal. The question is: How do you translate the information recorded on the rubric into a grade that will clearly show whether a student achieved mastery or not?

Translating the Rubric Into a Grade

You are probably thinking, "Why does there need to be a chapter regarding grading?" After all, is that not what we have been doing this entire time by creating rubrics and using them to evaluate students? Being able to translate the rubric into an accurate grade is part of the validity process. If the grade does not properly reflect student achievement, then the rubric is invalid. That is why it is so important to determine how the rubric will translate to the gradebook.

In a perfect world, report cards would not reflect a letter or number grade. Instead, they would display the level of mastery the student has achieved. This mastery-based grading does not put the student work in the hierarchy of a letter scale. Instead, it puts the bar at mastery of the learning objective and then determines whether students have met that bar, whether they are moving toward it but not quite there yet, or, in some cases, whether students exceed the bar and take it to another level.

With mastery-based grading, a rubric might look like Figure 38. This rubric makes the grading easier because you, as the teacher, evaluate whether students mastered the skill or they did not. There is no percentage, no points, and no GPA to determine. You would simply indicate on the report card the learning objectives students have mastered, those they have exceeded with greater depth of understanding, or those that still need further teaching before mastery can be gained. Is that not how life works? You either show mastery of a skill—whether it be doing a report at work, successfully figuring out your taxes, changing a headlight bulb in your car, or baking cookies—or you do not. Occasionally, you might exceed and make the most delicious chocolate chip cookies ever, or the report impresses your boss so much that you get a promotion, but, most times, the task is either mastered or it is not. That headlight is either installed correctly and works, or it does not. The IRS is not sending your taxes back to you with a grade and a sticker praising your work. If you do not master those, you could end up getting audited. The point is that, if we are trying to get children ready for the real world, mastery grading would be the most effective because once you graduate school, rarely are you ever given a letter grade on your performance. You are assessed for mastery.

The Letter Grade

Unfortunately, with colleges needing to have a GPA in order for admission, the reality is that, in a lot of cases, a rubric has to be translated into a letter grade. This letter grade, much like the rubric itself, is supposed to communicate whether a student attained mastery. There are various ways you can go about translating a rubric into a letter grade.

One option is to turn the rubric score into a percent by dividing the number of points earned by the possible total. Figure 39 is an example of a rubric for assessing a group project that details specific points. Notice that under "Presentation Techniques," a majority of specific performance objectives were determined to be "Excellent," but one aspect was "Good," making the grade a 9 rather than a 10. The same goes for "Time and People Management;" however, this category still averages out as a high "Needs Improvement," or a 6. Using the weighted scale at the bottom, which places more relevance on the "Content," "Art Component," and "Presentation Techniques," rather than "Time and People Management," gives this particular group an 87, which, according to our conversion scale, is a B on the performance. Although this group did not do so well on "Time and People Management," the score did not pull down the evaluation of the true learning objectives, which are

Rubric for Discovery Unit

Students: _____   **Topic:** _____

	Content	Presentation	Group Work
Exceeds (E)	✓ Students teach the information in the standard in depth, providing a deep understanding that goes beyond the standard's content. ✓ Students are clear in their teaching of the content, providing examples and detail to help with understanding. ✓ The questions the group provides capture all aspects of the standard.	✓ Student presentation is well organized, with group members' aware of their roles and what is being taught. ✓ Visual and handouts that the group uses bring meaning to the presentation and are well explained. ✓ Students are confident in their speaking ability and are easily heard by the audience.	✓ Students work well with one another, listening to each other's ideas and allowing all to contribute. ✓ Students are on task as a group, working with focus and getting tasks done when needed. ✓ Students do a great job of incorporating everyone's strengths into the design of the presentation.
Mastery (M)	✓ Students teach the information in the standard at a surface level, providing the basics but not a deep understanding. ✓ Students provide examples and detail to help with understanding, but more are needed. ✓ The questions the group provides capture most aspects of the standard.	✓ Student presentation is organized, but some group members are not aware of their role or there is a moment of confusion. ✓ Visual and handouts that the group uses bring a basic understanding to the presentation but need to be explained better for a deep understanding. ✓ Students are confident in their speaking ability but are not always heard by the audience.	✓ Students work well with one another, but don't always listen to each other's ideas and allow all to contribute. ✓ Students are on task as a group, working with focus and getting tasks done most of the time. ✓ Students do a good job of incorporating everyone's strengths into the design of the presentation most of the time but not always.

FIGURE 38. Sample mastery-based grading rubric.

	Content	Presentation	Group Work
Progressing (P)	✓ Students do not teach the information in the standard, missing the concept they should address. ✓ Students do not provide examples and detail to help with understanding. ✓ The questions the group provides do not capture the aspects of the standard.	✓ Student presentation is disorganized, with many group members unsure of their role and what is being taught. ✓ Visual and handouts that the group uses do not bring meaning to the presentation and seem off topic. ✓ Students are not confident in their speaking ability.	✓ Students do not work well with one another; they do not listen to each other's ideas and allow all to contribute. ✓ Students are not on task as a group, lacking focus and not able to get tasks done. ✓ Students do not do a good job of incorporating everyone's strengths into the design of the presentation.

FIGURE 38. Continued.

Multicultural Project Presentation Rubric

Students: _____   Topic: _____

	Content	Art Component	Presentation Techniques	Time and People Management
Excellent (9–10)	✓ Issue is clearly stated and provides focus for the entire presentation. ✓ Main points are strongly supported with much specific evidence. ✓ Presentation flows logically, with a clear beginning, middle, and end.	✓ Art is thoroughly integrated into the presentation. ✓ Art adds meaning to presentation content. ✓ Art is designed in a professional manner. ✓ Art can clearly be viewed.	✓ All participants speak with appropriate volume, speed, diction, and enthusiasm. ✓ Participants maintain good eye contact. ✓ Presentation appears well rehearsed and transitions are clear. ✓ Presenters capture audience's attention and generate enthusiasm.	✓ Presentation is completed in the recommended time allotment (10–15 min.). ✓ All team members contribute equally.
Good (7–8)	✓ Issue is stated at the beginning, but focus strays occasionally. ✓ Main points are supported with some specific evidence. ✓ Presentation flows logically but lacks a clear introduction and/or conclusion.	✓ Art is separate from, but referred to in, the presentation. ✓ Art supports the content. ✓ Design is adequate. ✓ Art cannot clearly be viewed by all.	✓ Participants generally speak with appropriate volume, speed, diction, and/or enthusiasm. ✓ Participants maintain occasional eye contact. ✓ Presentation is organized but lacks precise transitions. ✓ Presenters keep audience engaged.	✓ Presentation is slightly long/short in use of time. ✓ All team members contribute, but unequally.

FIGURE 39. Sample graded rubric.

	Content	Art Component	Presentation Techniques	Time and People Management
Needs Improvement (0–6)	✓ Issue is weak and/or loses focus in the presentation. ✓ Presentation lacks details and specific evidence. ✓ Presentation appears random, lacking a clear beginning, middle, and end. Points: 10 x 3 = 30	✓ Art is an afterthought or overlooked in the presentation. ✓ Art detracts from the content. ✓ Art is sloppy and/or seems thrown together. ✓ Art cannot be clearly viewed. Points: 8 x 3 = 24	✓ Participants frequently do not speak with appropriate volume, speed, diction, or enthusiasm. ✓ Participants rarely maintain eye contact. ✓ Presentation appears unrehearsed and disorganized. ✓ Presenters do not engage audience. Points: 9 x 3 = 27	✓ Presentation time is significantly cut off. ⊘ Not all team members contribute. Points: 6 x 1 = 6

Overall Rubric Total: 87

FIGURE 39. Continued.

weighed more heavily. Similarly, if the group had scored highly on "Time and People Management" but did poorly on the "Art Component," this would not inflate the group's grade, but rather show a truer picture of the students' mastery of the learning goals.

A second option is to create a range of points. To do so, you would determine the total points possible and then divide that by 5 to create the different levels of the range. Dividing by 5 gives you five ranges, one for each of the letter grades. An easy example would be if you had a rubric that was worth a total of 30 points. Dividing by 5, you would have a six-point range for each letter grade meaning:

✓   24–30 = A
✓   18–23 = B
✓   12–17 = C
✓   6–11 = D
✓   0–5 = F

Figure 40 is an example of what a rubric worth 10 points might look like. The nice thing about having a range is that there is a little bit of space for a teacher to give his opinion, but the parameters of the range keep his opinions from becoming too subjective. For instance, this rater circled both of the specific performance characteristics in "Animals/Plants." The range was 4–0, meaning the rater could have scored this a 4, 3, 2, 1, or 0. This rater determined the student work was near the top of the progressing work range and scored the student a 3.

A third option for grading is the even-steven method. In this, all categories are weighted the same and there is no range of performance. This option provides the most objective grade, but it also takes away any flexibility, as the rubric completely determines the overall grade. Figure 41 is an example rubric template that uses this method: Once the rater has made her decision about which box to check, the score is automatically determined. However, if we used a straight conversion, the student here would have a total of 11 points out of 16, which would be a 68%. On a traditional scale this would be a D, but you would hardly think this performance to be in the D range, given that one of the stated objectives was "Exemplary," while another was "Accomplished." If you were to make a grading scale using just the numbers, it would look like this:

✓   All 4s = 100%
✓   All 3s = 75%
✓   All 2s = 50%
✓   All 1s = 25%

As you can see, this scale is sort of unrealistic. Students either get an A (100%) or a C (75%)—there is no in between. And both of the bottom ratings result in a failure. How does one get a more accurate and objective score that matches the

Origami Ecosystem Rubric

Students: _____   Topic: _____

Overall	Content/Research	Animals/Plants	Ecosystem
Great Work (10–8)	1. Index cards include detailed explanations about how each plant/animal fits into the ecosystem 2. There is a clear picture of how the ecosystem works as a whole (3.) Sources seem to be reliable with complete documentation of where they came from	1. Origami feature 10 plants/animals from the ocean ecosystem 2. It is clear what plant/animal is being represented by the origami	1. Ecosystem looks professional and represents the ocean 2. Plants and animals are easy to see interacting in the ecosystem (3.) Ecosystem includes many other features besides just the plants/animals
Average Work (7–5)	(1.) Index cards are included, but the explanations of how each plant/animal fits into the ecosystem are not very detailed (2.) How the ecosystem works as a whole is explained in a basic manner, but a clear picture is not provided 3. Sources seem to be reliable, but there is incomplete documentation of where they came from	1. Origami feature 7–9 plants/animals from the ocean ecosystem 2. It is not always clear what plant/animal is being represented by the origami	1. Ecosystem represents the ocean but does not look professional (2.) Plants and animals are usually easy to see interacting in the ecosystem but not always 3. Ecosystem includes a few features besides just the plants/animals but could use more
Progressing Work (4–0)	1. 10 index cards are not provided, or they provide little to no detail of how each plant/animal fits into the ecosystem 2. How the ecosystem works as a whole is not explained 3. Sources do not seem reliable, or there is no documentation of where they came from	(1.) Origami feature six or fewer plants/animals from the ocean ecosystem (2.) Most of the time it is not clear what plant/animal is being represented by the origami	1. Ecosystem does not seem to represent the ocean or is very sloppy 2. Plants and animals are not easy to see interacting in the ecosystem (3.) Ecosystem does not include other features besides just the plants/animals
Total = 15 **C**	7/10	3/10	5/10

FIGURE 40. Example 10-point rubric.

Analytic Scoring Rubric					
	Beginning 1	Developing 2	Accomplished 3	Exemplary 4	Score
Criteria #1	Description reflecting beginning level of performance	Description reflecting movement toward mastery	Description reflecting achievement of mastery	Description reflecting highest level of performance	4
Criteria #2	Description reflecting beginning level of performance	Description reflecting movement toward mastery	Description reflecting achievement of mastery	Description reflecting highest level of performance	2
Criteria #3	Description reflecting beginning level of performance	Description reflecting movement toward mastery	Description reflecting achievement of mastery	Description reflecting highest level of performance	2
Criteria #4	Description reflecting beginning level of performance	Description reflecting movement toward mastery	Description reflecting achievement of mastery	Description reflecting highest level of performance	3

FIGURE 41. Sample rubric template for evenly weighted categories.

performance? First off, a teacher has to ask herself, is it really possible for a student to give a performance and truly get a zero? With a zero, you are claiming that the student learned absolutely nothing. Even the most reluctant student is going to learn something, even if he or she learns what not to do to get a good grade. As the teacher, you would want to set the bottom grade. For example, if a student got all 1s on this rubric, the lowest grade he could receive would be a 60%. This is not a great grade, but also not a GPA-killing zero. By setting this as the lowest, the grading scale changes completely. Now the grading scale looks like this:

✓ All 4s (16) = 100%
✓ All 3s (12) = 88%
✓ All 2s (8) = 72%
✓ All 1s (4) = 60%

There are, of course, scores that fall between these ranges. The rubric we first used for this example was an 11. That would mean this score would reflect a mid to low B. That is a huge difference from the D+ received before.

There is an online tool that will allow you to set the minimum passing grade as well as the number of ranges of performance and stated objectives. This can be found at https://roobrix.com. You simply enter in where the mark fell for each stated objective, and Roobrix will tabulate the grade for you.

Whichever method you choose is up to you, but remember that you want to choose the one that best reflects the student performance as compared to mastery of the learning objectives. That will ensure that the rubric is reliable.

Holistic Grade

Just as there is a holistic rubric, there is a holistic grade. If you watched a student performance and thought to yourself, "That is B work," that is how the performance should be reflected in rubric. The holistic is not as mathematical or precise as one that has a specific point breakdown, but there is a little room for teachers to decide what the appropriate grade is. Of course, by using this method you run the risk of grader bias, counting effort for or against the student, or other variables that cause subjectivity. As long as you draw some parameters and the specific performance objectives are clearly spelled out, the grade could be an accurate reflection of the student work.

Figure 42 is an example of a rubric using holistic grading. Without percentages or points, how do you determine the grade for this rubric? The score becomes an averaging of the grades. On the stated objectives where the grade is in a possible range, the teacher will have to decide where the student performance falls. It might look like this:

- ✓ Originality/Creativity = B
- ✓ Completeness = C
- ✓ Relevance/Quiz = A
- ✓ Understandability = D

Given that all of these categories are being equally weighed, this rubric assessment would be in the C range.

This method can be used on rubrics with multiple specific performance characteristics in the stated objectives. The same rubric just used could be broken down further (see Figure 43). This scoring does not have to be an exact science, but there does need to be a logic to it. A student cannot get two ratings of "Excellent" and one "Good" and be rated a B. The two A's would outweigh the lone B. You can elect to

Constitution Song Performance Rubric

Students: _____   Song: _____   Assigned Article: _____

	Poor (D–F)	Good (B–C)	Excellent (A)
Originality/ Creativity	Performers talk but just stand there doing nothing and show no enthusiasm. Song does not have any rhythm or catchiness, and/or the lyrics are not written by the group—they are from another source.	Song is somewhat catchy, and some of the group shows enthusiasm. Song is original but not overly clever. A prop may be used, but it is not used consistently to support the song's message.	Song is very catchy and original, even if the tune is from an existing song. Entire group is enthusiastic and into the performance. Group uses a prop in a creative manner.
Completeness	Song fails to cover any aspect of the assigned article. If main parts are covered, the interpretation is incorrect. There is no chorus, which should contain the central idea of the article from the Constitution.	Song covers some of the article, but other parts are left out or not covered well enough. Chorus is not repeated enough or does not contain the major idea of the article.	Song addresses entire article, and all of the article's main points are covered with detail and clarity. Chorus explains the major point of the assigned article and is repeated four times.
Relevance/Quiz	The quiz does not have five questions, or the questions have little or nothing to do with the main ideas of the song and/or article. Another possibility is the quiz is too easy, or the questions are not covered by the song. The quiz may be too easy with obvious answers or difficult with ridiculously challenging questions.	The quiz has five questions, but some of the questions have little or nothing to do with the article. Or, information in the questions is wrong, or some of the questions are not covered by the song. The quiz may have a question or two that are too easy or too challenging.	All five questions deal with the main points of the article. All of the questions are covered by the song in detail, and the quiz is challenging, but it is not too easy or too difficult.
Understandability/ Lyric Sheet	The lyrics are impossible to understand because the music is too loud or the words are spoken too quickly. No lyric sheet is provided, or it is illegible.	Some of the lyrics are hard to hear or do not make sense. Lyric sheet does not include all of the lyrics, or some of it is hard to read.	All of the lyrics are clear and easy to understand. The lyric sheet is either typed or neatly written.

FIGURE 42. Example completed holistic rubric.

Constitution Song Performance Rubric

Students: _____ Song: _____ Assigned Article: _____

Overall	Originality/Creativity	Completeness	Relevance/Quiz	Understandability
Excellent (A)	✓ Song is very catchy, causing you to be singing it in your head after the performance. ✓ Entire group is enthusiastic and into the performance. ✓ Lyrics are completely original, even if the tune is from an existing song.	✓ Entire article is addressed. ✓ Main points are covered with a good deal of detail and clarity. ✓ Chorus explains the major point of the assigned article and is repeated four times.	✓ All five of the questions deal with the main points of the article. ✓ All of the questions are covered by the song in detail. ✓ Quiz is challenging but is not too easy or difficult.	✓ All of the lyrics are clear and easy to understand. ✓ The lyric sheet is either typed or neatly written.
Good (B–C)	✓ The song is somewhat catchy in places. ✓ Some of the group shows enthusiasm, but not all. ✓ The song is original but not overly clever.	✓ Song covers some of the article, but other parts are left out or not covered well enough. ✓ Song does not contain the major idea of the article. ✓ Chorus is not repeated enough or does not contain the major idea of the article.	✓ Quiz has five questions, but some of the questions have little or nothing to do with the article. ✓ Some of the information in the questions is wrong or not covered by the song. ✓ Quiz may have a question or two that are too easy or too challenging.	✓ Some of lyrics are hard to hear or do not make sense. ✓ Lyric sheet does not contain all of the lyrics, or some of it is hard to read.

FIGURE 43. Example completed holistic rubric broken down into more objectives.

Overall	Originality/Creativity	Completeness	Relevance/Quiz	Understandability
Needs Work (D–F)	✓ Song does not have any rhythm or catchiness. ✓ Performers talk but just stand there doing nothing and showing no enthusiasm. ✓ Lyrics are not written by the group—they are taken from another source.	✓ Song fails to cover any aspect of the assigned article. ✓ If main parts are covered, the interpretation of the song is incorrect. ✓ There is no chorus, which should contain the central idea of the article from the Constitution.	✓ Quiz does not have five questions, or the questions have little or nothing to do with the main ideas of the song and/or article. ✓ Questions that make up the quiz are not covered by the song. ✓ Quiz may be too easy with obvious answers or difficult with ridiculously challenging questions.	✓ Lyrics are impossible to understand because the music is too loud or the words spoken too quickly. ✓ No lyric sheet is provided, or it is illegible.

FIGURE 43. Continued.

use minuses and plusses to make the averaging easier, but that would depend on the grading scale your school uses.

Anchor Grading

A good way to make sure your rubrics are reliable and valid is to use the practice of anchor grading. This involves multiple people using the same rubric to evaluate the same performance. If the rubric is written well and clearly shows what each level of the performance would look like, then the scores between these multiple raters will be close to one another. You do not want to have one evaluator who is a tough grader give a student a progressing score, while another, who is more lenient, scores the child as advanced.

You can begin to anchor your rubrics by assembling an anchoring team. This team can be made up of fellow teachers, students, or parents. The anchoring team all watch the same performance—that way there are not any miscellaneous variables. If need be, you can film the performance and let evaluators watch it at their leisure. Once everyone has completed the rubric and determined a grade, the team compares the results. Any disagreement is discussed to determine whether the rubric needs to be clearer or if it was simply a misunderstanding. It is important to have a few people on the anchoring team so that you are really testing the validity of the rubric.

Another way to anchor grade is to show the team a few performances and have the team members rank them from best to worst. Again, if someone sees one performance as the best and another rater thinks it is the worst, there may be something wrong with the objectivity of the rubric, and adjustments might need to be made to make these results more reliable.

You might also use exemplars to set the bar for each of the levels. If you have past performances, you can refresh your memory of how to evaluate by using them to guide you. For example, if you have three different ranges of performance in your rubric, keep an example or two from each of these. Review these to set in your mind what each range looks like.

Anchor grading is especially important if someone other than yourself is going to evaluate students using the rubric. For instance, let us say you are having students give a presentation to a panel of local business owners. You should have anchored the rubrics beforehand and made sure the language was clear and specific enough that it leads the scorers to be consistent with the grading. You should probably also provide a primer on how to use the rubric beforehand. Sitting down and walking raters through the rubric, or even having an anchoring session with them using a group's practice performance, might be a good way to get everyone on the same page.

Effective Feedback

When using a rubric to evaluate the performance of a student, in order for students to get something out of it that is more than just a number or a grade, you need to provide effective feedback. The rubric is not the end-all, be-all. The rubric merely acts as a communication tool that enables you to take the conversation and, thus, the learning further. The question becomes: What does effective feedback look like? Effective feedback is simply explaining the "why" of what you marked on the rubric. In other words, what is the evidence that led you to rate the student how you did?

When giving written feedback on a rubric, you need to consider what you say. Just as your specific performance characteristics need to "show" students, not "tell" them, your feedback needs to do the same. The rubric language and the feedback language should go hand in hand, complementing one another and adding dimension to the evaluation.

Here are some guidelines to follow that will enable your feedback to be as effective as possible:

- ✓ Write a comment for each of the specific performance characteristics you circle.
- ✓ Comments should, as much as possible, answer why you marked a criterion the way you did.
- ✓ Feedback should provide students with specific guidance as to what can be done to improve.
- ✓ If in the top tier, you should point out what students were successful at so that they can repeat it in future performances.
- ✓ Whenever possible, point to specific examples in the performance so that students know from where you are drawing your evidence.
- ✓ Feedback should be succinct but detailed.
- ✓ If more room is needed, considered using sticky notes or making notes on the back of the rubric.

Figure 44 is an example of a rubric that has been given written feedback. For every specific performance characteristics circled, there is an adjoining comment to go with it. Not only that, the comments point to specific instances in which the student could have improved the performance, such as the suggestion under "Presentation," where it was noted, "map good but other visuals could add additional content," or under "Content," where it says, "ideas [are] identified but not well

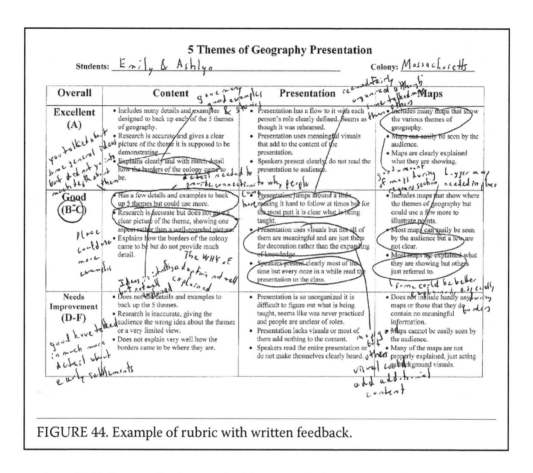

FIGURE 44. Example of rubric with written feedback.

explained." If the initial rubric is the blueprint for how to get a high range of performance, the comments made on the rubric are the blueprint for how to improve.

In addition, even if a student does place in the uppermost range of performance, pointing out what he or she did to achieve mastery is important. For example, under "Maps," the comment is made that "there was a good [number] of maps during Regan's section," and under "Content," the evaluator noted that the students "gave many good examples and stories." These comments bring the rubric to life. If you just circle the specific performance characteristic and leave it at that, students are given a sterile, lifeless document that may not be of any value to them.

How to Return Rubrics to Students

In addition to written feedback is the power of spoken feedback. This occurs when you return the rubric to students, which is actually one of the most important aspects of the rubric process. There are two ways to give the graded rubric back to students. The first one involves you handing them their rubrics, them glancing at the grade you have given them, and, many times, them leaving their rubric behind on their desks or pitching it in the recycling bin when the bell rings. The second involves you sitting down, one-on-one or as a group if the performance was a group one, and discussing the performance through the rubric. This is when part of the learning takes place. This is when students and the teacher reflect.

In order to do this, the teacher needs to have the opportunity to hold these conversations. That means having students either move on to the next project and, while they are working independently, sitting down and having these conferences, or this could involve setting up office hours during lunch or after school to be able to talk with students. Whichever method you choose, you have to give yourself 10 to 15 minutes to have the conversation. Sometimes it may be shorter, but the time needs to be provided in order to have the opportunity to allow the conversation to happen.

When you sit down to conference, you could start with the simple question of "How would you have rated yourself on this performance?" before even showing students the rubric grade. This acts as an anchoring of sorts. If the student thinks his performance was at the same level that you evaluated him at, then the conversation becomes about what you both saw, with the student providing insight on how to do a better job next time or what improvements can be made. If the student and teacher are way off on the evaluation, that becomes a conversation. What can the student say to convince the teacher of his point of view, and how can the teacher do the same? The learning process is revealed through these conversations. Interestingly, many times the student will be harder on himself than the teacher because he is aware of all of the opportunities he did not take, or all of the times when he did not give the best-quality work. You and the student will learn so much by having these conferences. You do not want to miss the opportunity by simply handing grades back.

Assessing This Chapter

To test what you learned about grading, use Reader Assessment 8 (on the following page).

READER ASSESSMENT 8

Grading Rubric 1

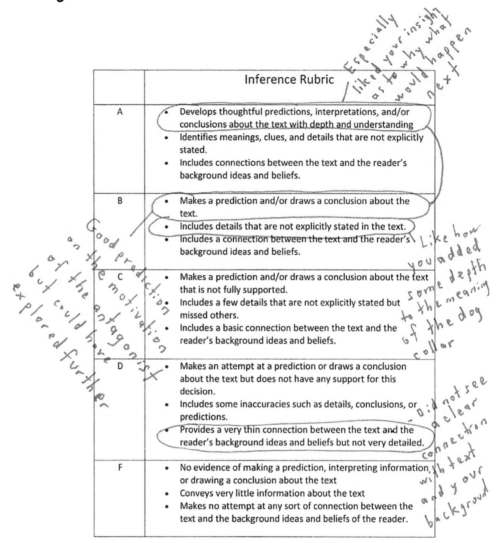

Inference Rubric

Especially liked your insight as to why what would happen next

A	• Develops thoughtful predictions, interpretations, and/or conclusions about the text with depth and understanding • Identifies meanings, clues, and details that are not explicitly stated. • Includes connections between the text and the reader's background ideas and beliefs.
B	• Makes a prediction and/or draws a conclusion about the text. • Includes details that are not explicitly stated in the text. • Includes a connection between the text and the reader's background ideas and beliefs.
C	• Makes a prediction and/or draws a conclusion about the text that is not fully supported. • Includes a few details that are not explicitly stated but missed others. • Includes a basic connection between the text and the reader's background ideas and beliefs.
D	• Makes an attempt at a prediction or draws a conclusion about the text but does not have any support for this decision. • Includes some inaccuracies such as details, conclusions, or predictions. • Provides a very thin connection between the text and the reader's background ideas and beliefs but not very detailed.
F	• No evidence of making a prediction, interpreting information, or drawing a conclusion about the text • Conveys very little information about the text • Makes no attempt at any sort of connection between the text and the background ideas and beliefs of the reader.

Good prediction on the motivation of the antagonist but could have explored further

Like how you added some depth to the meaning of the dog collar

Did not see a clear connection with text and your background

Anchored score: This student would probably receive a C for her essay. The reason is that the first specific performance characteristic of making a prediction is split between an A and a B. The overall evaluation was a B, but the rater wanted to make sure that he pointed out that one particular example was very insightful and deserved an A, making this probably a B+. This also gives the student something to shoot for with the rest of her examples. The second, which covers details not specifically mentioned in the text, seems to squarely be in the B range. Note that the comment does point out how the student could have improved her score. As for the final one concerning the connection between the text and student's own background, the student seems to have either misunderstood or not been sure what that looked like because the rater did not detect a clear connection to it. That gives us three grades:

- ✓ B+ = First specific performance characteristic
- ✓ B = Second specific performance characteristic
- ✓ D = Third specific performance characteristic

This would more than likely average out to a C, maybe a C+ if the grading scale involves pluses and minuses.

Grading Rubric 2

Playing Store

Overall	Store	Mathematics
(E)	✓ The invoice is filled out in detail, indicating everything that was sold, for how much, and how many. ✓ Store looks professional with clearly marked prices and an organized setup that makes it easy for people to shop. ✓ Five sales are offered and show a variety of different percentages.	✓ The discount from sales is calculated correctly for all items. ✓ The tax for purchases is calculated correctly. ✓ Register funds balance with the receipt perfectly, matching the inventory sold with the cash in the drawer.
(M–P)	✓ The invoice is filled out, indicating everything that was sold, for how much, and how many, but lacks detail, making it difficult to understand clearly. ✓ Store looks fairly organized with marked prices and a setup that makes it easy for people to find most things but not all. ✓ Five sales are offered but show a limited variety of different percentages.	✓ The discount from sales is calculated correctly for most of the items but not all. ✓ The tax for purchases is calculated correctly for most items but not all. ✓ Although the register funds do not balance perfectly, the receipt is only $5 or less either above or below the inventory sold with the cash in the drawer.

Overall	Store	Mathematics
(L)	✓ The invoice is filled but does not include everything that was sold, for how much, and how many. ✓ Store does not look professional, not indicating prices clearly, or is so unorganized that it makes it difficult for people to shop. ✓ Fewer than five sales are offered or are all the same percentage for the discounts.	✓ <u>The discount from sales is not calculated correctly, either giving too much of a discount or not enough.</u> ✓ The tax for purchases is not calculated correctly for many of the items. ✓ The register funds do not balance perfectly, and the receipt is more than $5 either above or below the inventory sold with the cash in the drawer.

Comments on the back:
✓ Good attention to detail on your invoice, clearly laying out what was sold and how much of it
✓ I had trouble locating the apples you had for sale, not easy to find
✓ Four of your sales were 50% off. Need to have more variety
✓ For your cookies, you were offering 25% off a price of $5.00, and yet you rang it up for $2.50, meaning you gave them 50% off. Your sale of grapes also not correct, nor the coffee
✓ Tax calculations done correctly
✓ Your register was $2.17 short. Not bad, but organize money so it is easier to count

Anchored score: This is a mastery-based scoring scale, meaning:
✓ E = Exceeds
✓ M = Met
✓ P =Progressing
✓ L = Limited

For the stated objective of the store, the three specific performance characteristics are one E, a P for the second one because the rater could not find the apples, and an M for the final one. That would put the performance in the M range. Under "Mathematics," the first specific performance characteristic is an L due to three mistakes out of a possible five, which is not a good ratio. The second one has the taxes correct, giving the student an E, while the third one is most likely in the P range because the student was a little short on the register, but also, it was not organized. That means the overall stated objective would be in the P range. Because the stated objectives are weighed equally, an M and a P could be averaged to a M- or a P+. If the grading scale does not have plusses or minuses, then it either has to be an M or a P. The teacher would have to review his comments to determine which side it goes to. Out of the six comments, four were pointing out mistakes, meaning the rater would fall toward the P range.

Grading Rubric 3

Photo Presentation Rubric

	Content	Photo Component	Pres. Techniques	Time and People Management
9–10	(✓) Issue is clearly stated and provides focus for the entire presentation. (✓) Main points are strongly supported with relevant details. ✓ Photos strongly support all subtopics.	✓ Photo component clearly supports the **global** issue. ✓ Shows originality. ✓ Well designed and can be clearly viewed. (✓) Have at least five appropriate photos, including at least one digital photo.	✓ Participants spoke clearly and effectively. ✓ Participants maintained good eye contact. ✓ Presentation flowed. ✓ Presentation was engaging.	✓ Completed in recommended time allotment (10 min.). ✓ Each team member described at least one photo's relationship to the main topic.
7–8	✓ Issue is stated at the beginning, but focus may stray. ✓ Main points are supported with some detail. (✓) Photos reflect most subtopics.	✓ Photo component supports **global** issue. (✓) Shows some originality. (✓) Design is adequate, but may not be easily viewed. ✓ Have five photos, but **not** all project requirements are met (BW/digital).	✓ Participants spoke somewhat clearly. ✓ Participants maintained occasional eye contact. ✓ Presentation was organized, but lacked precision. (✓) Presentation was somewhat engaging.	(✓) Ran slightly long or short. (✓) All team members contributed, but very unbalanced participation.

	Content	Photo Component	Pres. Techniques	Time and People Management
0–6	✓ Issue is weak and/or may lose focus in the presentation. ✓ Supporting details are unclear or ineffective. ✓ Little or no correlation between subtopics and photos.	✓ Photos do not support the **global** issue effectively. ✓ Show no originality. ✓ Cannot be viewed clearly. ✓ Have fewer than 5 photos.	✓ Participants did not speak clearly. ⊘ Participants rarely maintained eye contact. ⊘ Presentation lacked organization. ✓ Presentation was not engaging.	✓ Ran significantly long or short. ✓ Not all team members contributed.
	Points: _____ x 3 = _____	Points: _____ x 4 = _____	Points: _____ x 2 = _____	Points: _____ x 1 = _____

Anchored score: This is a rubric that uses specific numbers to determine the rating. Averaging the content, with two high placements and one middle, this would equal a 9. The photo component had two in the high range and two in the middle. Notice that the lack of comments makes it difficult to decide how to break this tie. It is unclear where exactly these components fell in their range of performance. But with the bolded global, it would lead one to assume this was a pretty important aspect, meaning the tie goes up to the 9. The presentation technique had one in the middle and two in the lower range. Again, a lack of comments makes it difficult to decide how bad the lower ranges were, but this would probably be in the 5–6 range. The time and people management has both in the middle range, but the lack of comments does not point us to whether this is a 7 or an 8, making it more a guess and subjective. Comments would break those ties much easier and in a more objective manner.

	Content	Photo Component	Pres. Techniques	Time and People Management
	Points: 9 x 3 = 27	Points: 9 x 4 = 36	Points: 6 x 2 = 12	Points: 8 x 1 = 8

When you take the weighing into consideration, the photo component having the greatest weight of 4, meaning its score would be multiplied by that number, as well as content and presentation techniques, the total score for this would be an 83 which makes this a B.

Hopefully, when you scored, you found yourself in the same general range as these. That would indicate that you are in good shape when it comes to grading your own rubrics.

Developing Rubrics for "Unmeasurable" Skills

From a math assignment, to a science lab, to an essay, to a mock trial, rubrics can be made to measure just about anything. Therein lies the beauty of rubrics.

For example, a real-world, authentic task might involve cooking a meal. Figure 45 is a rubric to determine whether a student knows how to prepare and cook a meal. If you gave a student a multiple-choice test on this same learning objective, the student could certainly display knowledge of how to make a meal. This does not, however, mean that he can actually make one. Cooking a meal is a skill that must be shown. The same goes for a skill such as paying attention. Figure 46 is a self-assessment in which a student has used the rubric to determine her level of being able to pay attention. This is a very important skill to learn and not one that can be addressed by a standardized test.

The Seven Survival Skills

Wagner (2008) identified seven survival skills for today's students:
1. critical thinking and problem solving,
2. collaboration across networks and leading by influence,
3. agility and adaptability,
4. initiative and entrepreneurialism,

Cooking Lab				
Beforehand: ✓ hand washing ✓ tying hair back ✓ equipment ready ✓ ingredients out ✓ everything is clean ✓ wearing an apron	Does not complete preparation.	Completes most of the tasks, but one or two are skipped.	Completes all of the steps but did not manage time well.	Practices good time management while completing all of the tasks.
Preparation: ✓ measuring ingredients properly ✓ reading the recipe ✓ missed a prep step	Does not complete most or completes none of the preparation steps.	Completes most of the preparation steps but missed one or more.	Completes all of the steps but did not manage time well.	Practices good time management while completing all of the tasks.
Cooking: ✓ attending to the stove ✓ controlling heat ✓ following instructions	Did not focus on the task.	Attempted tasks but got distracted.	Shows proper cooking methods but did not manage time well.	Shows proper cooking technique and professionalism.

FIGURE 45. Example cooking task rubric.

5. effective oral and written communication,
6. accessing and analyzing information, and
7. curiosity and imagination.

The problem, of course, is that a lot of students graduating college or high school do not possess these survival skills. Why is that? The focus on content standards, education data, and SMART goals has diminished the teaching of these skills in our school systems and colleges. The solution to this problem is to find proper ways to measure these very important skills. This chapter will explain the qualities of each of these skills and provide an example rubric for how each skill can be observed and measured in the classroom.

	🙁	😐	🙂
Attitude	I was grouchy with myself for not paying attention. I got grouchy with my classmates for telling me to pay attention.	I thought or said something mean to myself, such as "You're not good enough."	I encouraged myself to continue to pay attention. I looked at my rubric when I felt distracted.
Movement	I bumped into other kids many times. I sat in places where I would get distracted. I made noises with materials.	I bumped into other kids only a couple of times and usually apologized. I sometimes made good choices about where I was going to sit. I only made noises with materials once or twice.	I prevented myself from running into others. I chose spots where I would be able to pay attention the most. I used appropriate items to fidget with.
Focus	I forgot what to do most of the time. I did not listen to instructions.	I forgot what to do only a couple of times. I did not ask for help when I did not understand the directions.	I always asked for help when I did not understand the directions.
Ignoring Distractions	I paid more attention to the talking going on around me than to the class work.	I started to take part in distracting chatter but stopped myself.	I ignored all events going on around me that did not have to do with the lesson.
Chatting	I interrupted the class by chatting off task many times.	I made a couple of off-task remarks but then got back to work.	I never made an off-task remark. I stayed focused on the lesson.

FIGURE 46. Example student self-assessment.

Critical Thinking and Problem Solving

The ability to problem solve is a skill students will use the rest of their lives. Think about how valuable an employee with strong problem-solving skills is. Solving problems creatively and effectively saves money and leads to product development. The best way to train students in the classroom is to give them authentic tasks in which they can solve real-world problems.

Critical thinking, on the other hand, is being able to think at a higher level. According to Bloom's (1956) taxonomy, there are six levels of thinking:

1. remembering,
2. understanding,
3. applying,
4. analyzing,
5. evaluating, and
6. creating.

The first three—remembering, understanding, and applying—are considered lower level thinking skills. Can students recall information they have been told? Can students understand a concept or what a passage is telling them? Can students apply what they have learned to a different situation? We want all students to be able to function at these levels, but, unfortunately, in a lot of classrooms, this is the furthest the learning goes. There is no delving into the higher levels where critical thinking takes place. Can students analyze a reading and infer information that is not explicitly there? Can students evaluate a performance and give a clear explanation for what they used as their criteria and how they arrived at their opinion? Can students create something new? This is why rubrics and performance assessments are so valuable. It would be very difficult to show either of these skills on a traditional, multiple-choice assessment. They could, however, be shown in a performance.

Figure 47 is an example of a rubric that evaluates critical thinking skills. This could be used for any performance that calls on the use of these three higher level thinking skills, such as a persuasive essay, a problem-based learning assignment, or the analysis of a novel.

Collaboration

Students are going to be collaborating with others the rest of their lives—especially if they find themselves in any sort of business, there is collaboration with a boss, team members, or clients. Being able to work with others is a skill that will make these relationships stronger. That is why collaboration is such a valuable skill for students to learn.

	Analyzing	Creating	Evaluating
Deep Understanding of the Concept	Student is able to use specific inductive and deductive reasoning to make accurate and insightful inferences.	Student insightfully is able to take ideas from multiple sources and creates a new solution.	Student can make an insightful argument with logical reasons for support.
Pretty Good Grasp	Student is able to use logical reasoning to make inferences, but not necessarily deductive.	Student accurately is able to take ideas from multiple sources and create new solutions, but not necessarily insightful.	Student can make an appropriate argument with logical reasons for support, but not thought-provoking.
Surface-Level Understanding	Student is able to use superficial reasoning to make inferences, but no depth to it.	Student is able to take ideas from multiple sources, but not always accurate in how it is used to create the new solution.	Student makes an argument but is not always logical and/or supported.
Still Has Some Work to Do	Student makes unsupported and illogical inferences.	Students is not able to take information from multiple sources, or information is inaccurate and does not support the final solution.	Student either has difficulty making an argument or the argument is not logical or inaccurate.

FIGURE 47. Sample critical thinking skills rubric.

Collaboration is something that the teacher can evaluate, but sometimes a more insightful evaluation will come from the very people the student is collaborating with, as well as the student himself. You could use a rubric like Figure 48 to allow students to conduct peer and self-evaluations that determine how well someone is collaborating. You, the teacher, can evaluate this skill as well (see Figure 49).

Ultimately, being able to collaborate well is going to make for better outcomes in the classroom. Because you are working with students on the ability to collaborate, one natural byproduct is that you will be teaching students leadership skills. This results in students who have the confidence to step forward, share ideas, openly

Part of the Lesson	Self Ronnie	Peer Bobby	Peer Ricky
Research	3 - I found a bunch of research on volcanos but could've found more	4 - Showed us where some great websites were & found the most information	2 - Researched some but was also playing on-line games
Preparation	2 - I wasn't too helpful during this part but gave a few ideas	4 - Had the idea for how to display the volcano & built most of it	4 - Came up with the materials & helped to organize notes
Exhibit	3 - Typed up some of the info. sheets but misspelled a couple of terms	4 - Typed up most of the info. sheets for the board & printed photos	3 - Helped to design the tri-fold but forgot to bring in border
1 – Does not contribute to the group, actually holds it back.	2 – Does little to contribute to the group but occasionally helps.	3 – Contributes to the group in a positive manner and helps to make it better.	4 – Contributes mightily to the group, leading by example and making it better.

FIGURE 48. Sample peer/self-evaluation rubric.

and willingly listen to others' ideas, and inspire others to accomplish great things. Collaboration is an essential skill to have for any student.

Adaptability

Adaptability is one's ability to react to change. This is a valuable survival skill because we are developing technology at breakneck speed. It does not take more than a year or two to develop the newest technology that makes the old one obsolete. Those who are able to adapt to these changes often find much success. Those who are not able to keep up might find their skill set diminish. This is why doctors, lawyers, teachers, and people in almost any profession must continue learning throughout their careers; otherwise the techniques and procedures they use will become outdated. That is why adaptability is such an important skill to have in the real world.

How do we teach this in the classroom? We tell kids their entire lives that if they make a mistake, it is not a mistake if they learn from it. And yet how often in the classroom do we challenge students to fail? Give them a daunting task that will require them to take risks and try something that might result in glory or failure.

Overall	Design/Model	Collaboration
Excellent	Design clearly shows how the device will be built; it is labeled with measurements and parts. Model looks somewhat like the design, but there have been effective improvements made.	Student made him- or herself a valuable member of the group by offering positive contributions to the group dynamic. Student contributed to his or her part of the lesson as well as others'.
Good	Design shows how the device will be built; it is labeled with measurements and parts in most cases but not all. Model looks somewhat like the design, but there have been improvements made, although not always effectively.	Student made him- or herself a valuable member of the group most of the time by offering positive contributions to the group dynamic, but a few times he or she was negative or a distraction. Student contributed to his or her part of the lesson but not a lot to others'.
Needs Improvement	Design does not show how the device will be built, with little to no labeling of measurements and parts. Model looks nothing like the design, or there have not been any significant improvements made to increase effectiveness.	Student did not contribute positively to the group dynamic, often times being negative or a distraction. Student did not even contribute to his or her part of the lesson.

FIGURE 49. Sample collaboration rubric.

The way to teach failure is to facilitate lessons without a ceiling on them—lessons that allow students to try something new, something risky. How students adapt to this failure is where the true learning takes place. How many life-defining moments have happened to you as the result of failing at something and then learning from it? We want our students to be comfortable with the prospect of failure and that it can be a learning opportunity. This way, when failure undoubtedly happens in the real world, these children are not shocked by it but have developed strategies for how to adapt.

You could use a rubric such as Figure 50 to measure adaptability.

Adaptability Rubric

Student:_____

Indicate student's skills spectrum by placing the date on the line in the appropriate place.

Adaptability	Exceeding	Meeting	Progressing
Explores and Experiments	Eagerly takes on new challenges, has the initiative to learn independently, and tries innovative approaches to tasks.	Takes on new challenges, is willing to learn independently, and tries varied approaches to tasks.	Takes on assigned challenges, sometimes is willing to learn independently, and/or tries varied approaches to tasks from time to time.
←			
Works Effectively Through Changing Priorities	Proactively anticipates challenges and potential changes, is able to overcome obstacles by being innovative.	Independently will anticipate challenges and potential changes, is able to figure out a way to overcome obstacles.	Recognizes challenges with some assistance, sometimes gets stymied by obstacles.
←			
Views Failure as an Opportunity	Welcomes mistakes as a necessary part of learning and is able to rise above them.	Is comfortable with mistakes as part of the learning process and mostly is able to rise above them.	Sees the basic connection between mistakes and learning but not always able to rise above them.
←			
Draws From Strengths and Adapts Around Weaknesses	Recognizes strengths and weaknesses of self and others and is able to use these to an advantage.	Usually recognizes strengths and weaknesses of self and others but is not always able to use these to an advantage.	Occasionally recognizes strengths and weaknesses of self and others but is not usually able to use these to an advantage.
←			

FIGURE 50. Sample adaptability rubric.

Initiative

There are two types of people in the world: those who have to be told to do things and those who do not. Take brushing one's teeth, for example. When you are younger, your parents have to remind you nearly every night to make sure you do this. When a child eventually figures out for herself that she needs to brush her teeth because of the benefits of doing so, this is taking initiative. There are some kids who come to this realization earlier than others, and some who take longer, but eventually a good majority of people begin to take this initiative for themselves. The same happens in our school system. We spend a lot of time in the early years telling students what to do—bring a pencil, don't talk, write your assignment down in your log, make sure you get your assignment turned in, etc. The idea is that by the time they are in high school, students have begun to take the initiative themselves to complete basic tasks. This is true with some students and not so true with others.

Traditional methods like the ones listed previously do not teach a student initiative. Some activities that do help children to learn the skill include the following:

- ✓ Give students more choice because this gives them internal rewards, rather than doing the work because they will get a gold star or the approval of the teacher.
- ✓ Lessons need to be more authentic and take place in the real world so that students understand the context of what they are learning and how it might be used in their own lives.
- ✓ Give students longer term projects so that they build endurance and learn the valuable lesson that when the going gets tough, the tough get going.
- ✓ Allow students to solve their own problems. Many times, as the adult, we are quick to step in and offer a solution when students struggle. Giving them more opportunities to do this for themselves teaches initiative.
- ✓ Stop waving prizes and rewards in front of students to get them to do work. This only teaches them to wait for someone to offer another prize. Students need to see the value in who they are, not what they do.
- ✓ Most importantly, model initiative for students in the classroom. If they see their teacher taking initiative, they can make connections between what they see and what they can do about it.

How valued would a person be to his employer if he takes initiative and does not need to be watched to make sure he is working? Would not you, as the teacher, want a classroom full of these students? You would be able to do what is every teacher's dream: teach. You would have the ability to move around the classroom and work with students individually, allowing them to grow to their potential rather than waiting for the common denominator of the class to catch up. When you provide students with the freedom of self-directed learning, you get amazing results.

Students are more motivated because they have choice in what they are doing rather than being directed. And students can be more imaginative because they are not constrained by as many requirements. By showing initiative, they get into the higher levels of thinking you want students to achieve.

One way to measure initiative is by giving students a long-term project and lots of choices. The choices that students make will often times determine their level of initiative. If they make choices that are going to challenge them or allow them to become better learners, then they are showing initiative. Figure 51 is an example of a one-point rubric that gives the teacher room to indicate when a student has shown initiative.

Notice that there is plenty of room in the initiative column to add when a student went above and beyond the mastery. For instance, if a student showed a lot of initiative in the quality row, the teacher might report it like in the example in Figure 52.

Initiative can definitely be measured in the classroom but only if students are given lessons that allow them to show it. You cannot give students 10 math problems and then expect them to show initiative. You could, however, give them the choice to take the concept from those 10 problems and create problems of their own. If you merely assign students to all read the same book, it would be hard to show initiative other than with the pace with which the students read. However, if you are covering a theme such as isolation and you give the students three choices for a reading assignment—*Robinson Crusoe* (158 pages), *Lord of the Flies* (368 pages), and *Life of Pi* (430 pages)—you give the students an opportunity to show initiative if they do not simply choose a book based on how short it is, but rather select the one that seems more challenging. Students have a funny way of giving you what you ask for, so sometimes you have to offer them more opportunities to show this initiative.

Written and Oral Communication

The ability to communicate effectively with others is a valuable skill for any person to possess. One of the major reasons is that not everyone is able to do it. If you are someone who can do it and do it well, that is an advantage over others. There are two major ways to communicate—orally and through writing. Written communication can be displayed in a lot of different ways. Some examples include a short answer to a prompt, a persuasive essay, and a full-blown research paper. Figure 53 is an example of a rubric that evaluates the written communication of a creative writing piece for language arts in middle school through high school.

Written communication is not just found in language arts class, however. It can be put on display in math as well. We often tell students to show their work in math. Some argue that this is not necessary. As long as students get the correct

	Shows Progress	Shows Mastery	Shows Initiative
Product		Product meets the requirements of the learning objective and shows that the student has an understanding of it.	
Time Management		Student turned in all materials by the deadline and paced self well, getting a little done every day.	
Quality		Product is of a good quality, showing that the student put effort into meeting the stated requirements.	

FIGURE 51. Sample one-point initiative rubric.

		Shows Mastery	Shows Initiative
Quality		Product is of a good quality, showing that the student put effort into meeting the stated requirements.	*It is obvious a lot of thought and effort was put into the product, more than what the lesson called for. I was especially impressed with your attention to detail and the fact that you spent so much time creating a beautiful cover.*

FIGURE 52. Sample rubric snippet for quality category and teacher comments.

answer, what does it matter? What these students don't understand is that by showing their work, they are clearly communicating to the teacher their level of mastery. The teacher can see the thought processes they went through, the trial and error of

Overall	Clarity	Grammar/Spelling	Revision
Excellent (A)	✓ Writing piece has a clear beginning, middle, and end, with clear event sequencing. ✓ Writing piece consistently shows with descriptive words and sentences rather than tells the story. ✓ Sentence structure is consistently clear and easy for the reader to follow.	✓ Writing piece has few to no spelling/grammatical errors. ✓ Writing piece uses capitalization correctly consistently. ✓ Writing piece is typed in the correct format.	✓ Student turns in both a rough draft and a final draft along with detailed notes taken from the workshop. ✓ Student made several good revisions to the final draft based on the information received in the workshop. ✓ Between the rough and final draft, student was consistently able to expand, combine, and reduce sentences for meaning, reader/listener interest, and style.
Good (B–C)	✓ Writing piece has a beginning, middle, and end, but the sequencing is not always clear. ✓ Writing piece shows with descriptive words and sentences rather than tells the story for the most part, but there are a couple of occasions where action is told. ✓ Sentence structure for the most part is clear and easy for the reader to follow, but there are a few confusing sentences.	✓ Writing piece has some occasional spelling/grammatical errors. ✓ Writing piece uses capitalization correctly but not always consistently. ✓ Most of the writing piece is typed in the correct format, but a few guidelines are not followed.	✓ Student turns in both a rough draft and a final draft along with sparse notes taken from the workshop. ✓ Student made revisions to the final draft based on the information received in the workshop but overlooked some that needed to be made. ✓ Between the rough and final draft, student was able to expand, combine, and reduce sentences for meaning, reader/listener interest, and style, but not consistently throughout the piece.

FIGURE 53. Sample written communication rubric.

Overall	Clarity	Grammar/Spelling	Revision
Needs Improvement (D–F)	✓ Writing piece does not have a beginning, middle, and end because the sequencing is not very clear. ✓ Writing piece does not show with descriptive words and sentences; instead it tells the story. ✓ Sentence structure is not clear and easy for the reader to follow.	✓ Writing piece has many spelling/grammatical errors, causing it to be difficult to read. ✓ Writing piece does not use capitalization correctly consistently. ✓ Much of the writing piece is not in proper format as laid out by the guidelines.	✓ Student turns in both a rough draft and a final draft but has no notes from the workshop. ✓ Student made little to no revisions to the final draft based on the information received in the workshop. ✓ Between the rough and final draft, student did not expand, combine, and reduce sentences for meaning, reader/listener interest, and style.

FIGURE 53. Continued.

the problem, and their ability to replicate this understanding to another problem that uses the same formula.

Effective oral communication is just as important as written, but not something that students are usually given as much opportunity to do. After all, how does one get good at oral communication? By having experiences in which he or she can publicly speak. The more opportunities you give your students to speak publicly without fear, the more comfortable they will become. Every experience you give them will provide that much more confidence in their ability. You build up this confidence over time until students are not only comfortable with public speaking, but also very good at it. Figure 54 is an example of a rubric that covers the skill of oral communication.

These opportunities should also be authentic. Having students speak in front of the class, where they know everyone and are more comfortable, is a good way to get started in a safe environment. However, eventually you want to put students in a situation that is not as comfortable by providing outside audience members or public forums. Oftentimes in the real world, people will have to give a presentation to their boss, colleagues, or a client. Giving students the chance to present to high-pressure audiences will help them to get ready for that, as well as give them valuable experience in public speaking. And learning what goes into a successful or effective public presentation is also important to teach. Help students understand the importance of body language, tone of voice, the use of visual aids, persuasiveness, and confidence. These are skills that students can work on and get better at, and they should be evaluated in your rubrics.

Accessing and Analyzing Information

Being able to access and analyze information comes down to the skill of information literacy. In simpler terms, this means the ability to conduct research, pull from the research the most pertinent and useful information, and then use this information to accomplish goals. In a classroom, this might look like a student researching the planet Mars for a science paper. The student has to locate books and websites that provide information and cull through to find what is best going to help him write his paper. Then, he must take the information and put it into his own words, while still maintaining the integrity of the information.

Like all survival skills, accessing and analyzing information is not just a skill for the classroom, it is a skill for life. Being able to determine where to access information efficiently and effectively is important if you are trying to find out whether a store is open or not. Being able to evaluate information both critically and competently also comes in handy when trying to discern which political candidate to vote for. Using information accurately and creatively would be beneficial if you have to

Students: _____

Defense   **Topic:** _____

Overall	Content	Structure	Presentation
Excellent (A)	✓ Includes many additional details and examples designed to support the resolution. ✓ Group is able to answer questions posed by other audience members with confidence.	✓ Opening is strong and sets up a clear defense. ✓ Closing adds additional points and reestablishes the importance of the resolution. ✓ Both opening and closing provide strong finishes, leaving the audience with something to think about.	✓ Group presents itself in a professional manner, showing maturity throughout the defense. ✓ Group consistently speaks with confidence. ✓ Group works effectively as a team, complementing each others' defense.
Good (B–C)	✓ Includes additional details and examples but needs more to offer complete support. ✓ Group is able to answer most questions posed by other members but stumbles occasionally.	✓ Opening is adequate and sets up a defense but does not stand out as being strong. ✓ Closing adds an additional point or two but not many and reestablishes the importance of the resolution. ✓ The opening or the closing, but not both, provides a strong finish, leaving the audience with something to think about.	✓ Most of the time, group presents itself in a professional manner but does not maintain this through the entire defense. ✓ Group speaks with confidence most of the time but is not consistent throughout. ✓ Group works effectively as a team for the most part but does not always present a unified defense.

FIGURE 54. Sample oral communication rubric.

Overall	Content	Structure	Presentation
Needs Improvement (D–F)	✓ Does not include many additional details and examples that would have supported the resolution. ✓ Group is not able to answer questions posed by audience members.	✓ Opening is weak, actually hurting the defense. ✓ Closing does not offer any additional points and/or does not reestablish the importance of the resolution. ✓ Both opening and closing do not give strong finishes, leaving the audience wondering if the defense is even over.	✓ Group does not present itself in a professional manner, showing a lack of maturity throughout the defense. ✓ Group does not speak with confidence in its defense, looking unsure. ✓ Group does not work effectively as a team, contradicting each others' defense.

FIGURE 54. Continued.

figure out how to change your shower head. This skill transcends the classroom, so being able to perform it with a certain level of competence and confidence will make students valuable members of the workforce. Any time you are doing purposeful research in the classroom, this is a skill that will be taught.

Research papers, lesson presentations, portfolios, and debates are just a few types of products that require information literacy. Many times, teachers assume students have already been taught the skill of information literacy, especially if you have older students. This is a skill that must be retaught often. Students may have developed bad habits, so reviewing the basics of how to conduct proper research can be helpful to students at any level. Research can be broken down into skills:

- ✓ how to craft a search using keywords,
- ✓ which search engines are the most effective,
- ✓ determining whether a website can be trusted or not,
- ✓ how to synthesize information in your own words and properly cite your source to avoid plagiarism, and
- ✓ taking this information and using it to strengthen a position or argument.

These skills then can be measured using a properly written rubric, such as the example in Figure 55.

The more experience students get with information literacy, the better they are going to become at it. As the teacher, you need to make sure this exposure is guided so that through these experiences they are developing good practices rather than bad habits.

Curiosity

Learning is all about curiosity—whether that involves wanting to find out more information about a subject, reading a book that looks good, or trying a skill that sounds interesting. As babies, we are innately curious, wanting to explore and try everything. This curiosity is lost over time, and we must find opportunities to allow students to be curious. When classrooms focus too heavily on facts, recall, simple skills, and test-taking, students are not able to use their curiosity to motivate themselves to learn more. We need more inquiry-based learning, in which students can explore what they are curious about. In short, we need to develop ways for students to use their curiosity and imaginations in the classroom.

Performance assessments offer a whole set of possibilities that traditional testing does not. If students must write a song of their choice to teach others how to use a particular math formula, they will certainly have to use their imaginations. If you have students design and create their own experiment based on their own interests, this allows them to explore their curiosity. If students are able to write a

Research Paper

Students: _____   Topic: _____

Overall	Content	Research	Content
Excellent (90–100)	✓ Paper follows the outline clearly, allowing the reader to understand what is being discussed at any given time. ✓ Student provides plenty of examples to support statements made in the paper. ✓ Student includes 5–6 quotes from his or her research that add meaning to the paper.	✓ Various credible resources are used and included in the bibliography. ✓ Bibliography is correctly formatted using MLA style. ✓ Citations are used correctly throughout the paper.	✓ Research is consistently paraphrased/put into the student's own words. ✓ Expert interview is used throughout the paper, adding insight and depth to the information discussed. ✓ Student uses specific facts and data when necessary, giving the reader a clear understanding of the topic.
Good (70–89)	✓ Paper follows the outline, but doesn't always allow the reader to understand what is being discussed at any given time. ✓ Student provides examples to support statements in most cases, but not consistently. ✓ Student includes 5–6 quotes from his or her research, but they do not always add meaning to the paper.	✓ Sources are nearly all from the same medium. ✓ Bibliography has a few errors or has a few errors in the use of MLA style. ✓ Citations are used throughout the paper, and most are correct.	✓ Research is paraphrased/put into the student's own words most of the time. ✓ Expert interview is used sporadically throughout the paper, not providing much insight and depth to the information discussed. ✓ Student uses facts and data, but not always with enough specificity.

FIGURE 55. Sample research rubric.

Overall	Content	Research	Content
Needs Improvement (40–60)	✓ Paper does not follow the outline, causing confusion for the reader. ✓ Student provides few to no examples to support statements. ✓ Student includes fewer than 5–6 quotes from his or her research, or none add meaning to the paper.	✓ Sources lack credibility or variety. ✓ Bibliography has many errors in content and/or in use of MLA style. ✓ Citations are not used often or are used incorrectly throughout.	✓ Research is not paraphrased/put into the student's own words most of the time. ✓ Expert interview is barely used in the paper, not providing any insight and depth to the information discussed. ✓ Student does not use facts and data when necessary, leaving the reader with more questions than answers.

FIGURE 55. Continued.

creative piece instead of just a routine essay, they are able to tap into their curiosity to guide the assignment. If students debate the merits of the ideas expressed at the Constitutional Convention by role-playing as a person from that time period, they can be innovative in how they form their argument and present it.

Providing students with choice allows for much curiosity. The more choices we give students, the more chances they have to be curious. When we take these choices away, students receive a paint-by-numbers education, in which they follow directions, give the teacher what he wants, and are compliant. This environment does not foster curiosity.

How do you measure the skill of curiosity? You look for the characteristics that make up curiosity, such as if a student:

- ✓ likes to ask questions,
- ✓ gets excited about certain topics,
- ✓ is open to other ideas that makes him or her challenge his or her own,
- ✓ thinks outside of the box,
- ✓ enjoys problem solving,
- ✓ embraces the unpredictable,
- ✓ is willing to take risks,
- ✓ engages in dialogue with others,
- ✓ challenges the status quo, or
- ✓ dreams big.

In a rubric, assessing curiosity might look like Figure 56.

Creating the space for students to explore curiosity is very important, both physically and mentally. You can do this by building literal spaces in which students can explore and grow. Develop a classroom Makerspace in which students can build things and explore their curiosity. Makerspaces can take on a lot of different forms. Some can be very high-tech and include equipment such as 3-D printers, cutting devices, traditional hand tools, machines that can drill and shape complex parts, or other such industrial equipment. Makerspaces can also be simpler and include craft and art supplies, computers, electronic parts, building materials, and LEGOs. Whatever your budget, having a dedicated space in which students can explore their curiosity is good. Mental space means the teacher carving out the most important supply—time. Genius Hour is a great way to provide students with time to explore. Genius Hour stemmed from the same idea Google used with its employees in which it gave them 20% of their time to work on whatever they wanted to. This resulted in 50% of Google's new ideas being created from this time (Adams, 2016). This proves that learning and innovating does not always have to be structured and mandated in order to benefit students. Through Genius Hour, you give students an allotted set of time, say an hour a week, and allow them to pursue any passion or learn about anything they have been curious about. Genius Hour can be more guided by having

	Present	Displays Regularly	Lifelong
Open-mindedness	Is open to some unfamiliar ideas but not always	Is so open to unfamiliar ideas that when presented with them, compares and contrasts with own ideas	Seeks out other, contradictory opinions in order to broaden thinking
Asking Questions	Questions asked are more seeking to understand than to explore	Often asks thought-provoking questions that seek to explore	Questions most everything and hopes this stirring of the pot will lead to new ideas
Curiosity	Is interested in ideas in a narrow area of focus but not those outside of it	Is interested in most ideas and wants to explore further	Is so innately curious because loves learning and exploring new ideas
Risk-taking	Does not mind taking risks within reason, does not like to rock the boat	Is willing to take risks pretty regularly as long as it is accepted by others	Willing to take an unpopular point of view as long as it leads to further understanding
Motivation	Can get motivated if it is the right topic or idea but sometimes has to be prodded into it	Gets excited about ideas without much prodding and seeks answers for him- or herself	Gets really excited about new ideas to the point where it is difficult to stop exploring
Problem Solving	Tackles a problem when told to and thinks of a creative solution	Can come up with many possibilities for tackling a problem when given the chance	Wants to tackle a problem because curiosity compels him or her to

FIGURE 56. Rubric for assessing curiosity.

an essential question students must explore or a required final product. The main idea, however, is that students have time to explore their curiosity.

Assessing This Chapter

    The purpose of this chapter is to make you more comfortable with using—and creating—rubrics to evaluate hard-to-measure skills. Reader Assessment 9 (on the following page) is a self-assessment to determine the level at which you teach the survival skills in your classroom.

READER ASSESSMENT 9

Educator Self-Assessment	Critical Thinking and Problem Solving:	Collaboration:
	✓ Do you encourage students to go into more depth and explore ideas with deeper thinking? ✓ Do you ask students to create and ask their own essential questions? ✓ How often are students given the opportunity to solve authentic, real-world problems?	✓ Do you purposely teach students how to collaborate in your classroom? ✓ Do you provide opportunities for students to collaborate in various situations and with various people? ✓ Are students given the space and time to successfully collaborate with one another?
Adaptability: ✓ Do you accept change as normal and expect the same in your students? ✓ Are you and your students flexible in your thinking? ✓ Have you equipped your students with a variety of tools to solve problems?	**Initiative:** ✓ Do you coach students to push themselves to the next level? ✓ Do you provide opportunities for students to take risks? ✓ Is your classroom a place in which failure is an option?	**Effective Written and Oral Communication:** ✓ Do you provide lots of opportunities for students to share their voice in both written and oral formats? ✓ Do you coach students to have confidence in their written and oral communication? ✓ Are students encouraged to be clear in their written and oral communication?
Accessing and Analyzing Information: ✓ Do you provide students with the skills to effectively research? ✓ Do you have confidence that your students can do a competent Internet search and find reliable information? ✓ How often do you give students the chance to synthesize research into their own argument?	**Curiosity and Imagination:** ✓ Do you promote inquiry in your classroom? ✓ Are there opportunities for students to pursue their own interests? ✓ Do you encourage students to bring their own personal experiences to their learning?	How many of the survival skills do you confidently teach in your classroom?

Conclusion

Evaluating This Book

At this point in the book, you should have a very good understanding of how to create your own objective rubric. Your final assessment to gauge whether you have mastered these skills is to create a rubric that evaluates this book. Figure 57 is a template you might use.

Some suggestions for stated objectives include:
- ✓ clarity,
- ✓ organization,
- ✓ innovation,
- ✓ usefulness,
- ✓ thought-provoking,
- ✓ content,
- ✓ practicability,
- ✓ relevance,
- ✓ shareable, and
- ✓ helpfulness.

If you decide to undertake this task, send me your results, good or bad. They can be sent to me on Twitter @the_gifted_guy or through e-mail at thegiftedguy@yahoo.com. With your permission, I will post these on my website at https://www.

	Rubric for This Book		
Overall			
Excellent			
Good (But)			
Needs Improvement (Not)			

FIGURE 57. Book assessment rubric.

thegiftedguy.com. I also encourage you to post your evaluation of this book on Amazon or on the Prufrock Press website using your results from the rubric.

To help you with this evaluation, make sure you go back to the end of Chapter 3 and complete the rubric that you started there. This will give you a fairly accurate picture of your progression of mastery and what you truly learned from the book.

References

Abunassar, J., Kirkham, B., & Warkentin, E. (2015). *Co-constructing criteria.* Retrieved from https://evaluaryaprender.files.wordpress.com/2015/02/co-constructing-criteria-handout.docx

Adams, B. (2016). How Google's 20 percent rule can make you more productive and energetic. *Inc.* Retrieved from https://www.inc.com/bryan-adams/12-ways-to-encourage-more-free-thinking-and-innovation-into-any-business.html

Andrade, H. G. (1996). Understanding rubrics. *Educational Leadership, 54*(4), 14–18.

Bloom, B. (Ed.). (1956). *Taxonomy of educational objectives: The classification of educational goals. Handbook I: Cognitive domain.* New York, NY: Longmans Green.

Brookhart, S. M. (2013). *How to create and use rubrics for formative assessment and grading.* Alexandria, VA: ASCD.

Doyle, A. (2018). What are soft skills? *The Balance Careers.* Retrieved from https://www.thebalancecareers.com/what-are-soft-skills-2060852

Duckworth, A. L. (2016). *Grit: The power of passion and perseverance.* New York, NY: Scribner.

Duckworth, A. L., Peterson, C., Matthews, M. D., & Kelly, D. R. (2007). Grit: Perseverance and passion for long-term goals. *Journal of Personality and Social Psychology, 92,* 1087–1101.

Herman, J. L., Aschbacher, P. R., & Winters, L. (1992). *A practical guide to alternative assessment.* Alexandria, VA: Association for Supervision and Curriculum Development.

Huba, M. E., & Freed, J. E. (2000). *Learner-centered assessment on college campuses: Shifting the focus from teaching to learning.* Boston, MA: Allyn & Bacon.

Marzano, R. J. (2015). Using formative assessment with SEL skills. In J. A. Durlak, C. E. Domitrovich, R. P. Weissberg, & T. P. Gullotta (Eds.), *Handbook of social and emotional learning: Research and Practice* (p. 341). New York, NY: Guilford Press.

Miller, M. J. (2007). Reliability and validity. *Graduate Research Methods.*

The Mind Tools Content Team. (n.d.). *SMART Goals: How to make your goals achievable.* Retrieved from https://www.mindtools.com/pages/article/smart-goals. htm

National Governors Association Center for Best Practices, & Council of Chief State School Officers. (2010). *Common Core State Standards for English language arts.* Washington, DC: Author.

Ohio Department of Education. (2009). *Ohio Department of Education rubric for scoring music performance evaluation for grades K–12.* Columbus, OH: Author.

Stanley, T. (2014). *Performance-based assessment for 21st-century skills.* Waco, TX: Prufrock Press.

Stanley, T. (2017a). *10 performance-based projects for the math classroom.* Waco, TX: Prufrock Press.

Stanley, T. (2017b). *10 performance-based projects for the science classroom.* Waco, TX: Prufrock Press.

Stanley, T. (2018a). *10 performance-based STEM projects for grades 2–3.* Waco, TX: Prufrock Press.

Stanley, T. (2018b). *10 performance-based STEM projects for grades 6–8.* Waco, TX: Prufrock Press.

Wagner, T. (2008). *The global achievement gap: Why even our best schools don't teach the new survival skills our children need.* New York, NY: Basic Books.

Webb, N. L. (2002). *Depth-of-knowledge levels for four content areas.* Madison, WI: Wisconsin Center for Education Research.

About the Author

Todd Stanley is author of more than a dozen teacher-education books, including *Project-Based Learning for Gifted Students: A Handbook for the 21st-Century Classroom*, *Performance-Based Assessment for 21st-Century Skills*, and *When Smart Kids Underachieve in School: Practical Solutions for Teachers*. He was a classroom teacher for 18 years, teaching students as young as second graders and as old as high school seniors, and was a National Board Certified teacher. He helped create a gifted academy for grades 5–8, which employs inquiry-based learning, project-based learning, and performance-based assessment. He is currently the gifted services coordinator for Pickerington Local School District, OH, where he lives with his wife, Nicki, and two daughters, Anna and Abby. You can follow him on Twitter @the_gifted_guy or check out his website, where there are many free resources for educators, at https://www.thegiftedguy.com.

For Product Safety Concerns and Information please contact our EU
representative GPSR@taylorandfrancis.com
Taylor & Francis Verlag GmbH, Kaufingerstraße 24, 80331 München, Germany